WHAT PEOPLE ARE SAYING ABOUT MARY K. BAXTER'S BOOKS AND MINISTRY...

"Mary K. Baxter's books have reached around this world and have impacted people in all walks of life. As people get the opportunity to meet her and witness the power of God on her life, they learn it truly is *A Divine Revelation* from God."

—*T. L. Gabbard, Sr., Pastor, Wynne, Arkansas*

"Mary Baxter truly has an incredible testimony that needs to be shared with all. God surely is We have been blessed by Mary Baxter's ministry at our church....Hundreds have been saved and filled with the Holy Spirit, and many have been healed and set free."

—*Winford Walters, pastor, Elyria, Ohio*

"Mary Baxter has been a great blessing to our church family. Through her preaching abilities, many people have gotten saved and delivered, and a great number of backsliders have rededicated their lives back to God....I believe that her written testimonies will c'____ ____ lives of countless unbelievers and s____ ____ ____ ____ ____ any believers concernii____

—*Jason Alvai____* ____ *rsey*

A DIVINE
REVELATION
OF
DELIVERANCE

OTHER TITLES BY MARY K. BAXTER

A Divine Revelation of Angels
A Divine Revelation of Healing
A Divine Revelation of Heaven
A Divine Revelation of Hell
A Divine Revelation of Prayer
A Divine Revelation of the Spirit Realm
A Divine Revelation of Spiritual Warfare
The Power of the Blood
(all titles also available in Spanish)

OTHER TITLES BY GEORGE G. BLOOMER

Authority Abusers
Empowered from Above
Looking for Love (w/ teaching CD)
More of Him (w/ teaching CD)
Spiritual Warfare
Witchcraft in the Pews

MARY K. BAXTER
WITH GEORGE BLOOMER

A
DIVINE
REVELATION
OF
DELIVERANCE

**WHITAKER
HOUSE**

A DIVINE REVELATION OF DELIVERANCE

For speaking engagements, contact:

Evangelist Mary K. Baxter
Divine Revelation, Inc.
P.O. Box 121524
West Melbourne, FL 32912-1524
www.mbaxterdivinerevelation.org

George G. Bloomer
Bethel Family Worship Center
515 Dowd St.
Durham, NC 27701
www.bethelfamily.org

ISBN-13: 978-0-88368-754-3 • ISBN-10: 0-88368-754-2
Printed in the United States of America
© 2008 by Mary K. Baxter and George G. Bloomer

Whitaker House
1030 Hunt Valley Circle
New Kensington, PA 15068
www.whitakerhouse.com

Library of Congress Cataloging-in-Publication Data

Baxter, Mary K.
  A divine revelation of deliverance / by Mary K. Baxter; with George G. Bloomer.
    p. cm.
  Summary: "Describes the all-powerful deliverance of Jesus in overcoming Satan's plans for the deception, enslavement, and destruction of humanity"—Provided by publisher.
  ISBN-13: 978-0-88368-754-3 (trade pbk. : alk. paper)
  ISBN-10: 0-88368-754-2 (trade pbk. : alk. paper) 1. Spiritual warfare.
I. Bloomer, George G., 1963– II. Title.
  BV4509.5.B395 2008
  248.4—dc22
                                    2007041700

4 5 6 7 8 9 10 11 12 **UJ** 15 14 13 12 11 10 09

CONTENTS

PREFACE

J esus never promised that our lives would be void of challenges and trials. Some of our challenges come from God to test our faith and perfect our character. At other times, our trials are a decisive ploy by the enemy to catch us off guard and cause us to stumble from the foundation of God's Word. Often, many of the difficulties we encounter in the natural world are really a manifestation of the clash between the kingdom of God and the kingdom of darkness that is taking place in the invisible spirit realm.

For instance, all too often, members of the body of Christ and society in general suffer in silence as they struggle with habitual acts over which they feel they have no control, unaware of the root cause that drives their behavior. That cause is unseen evil forces from hell, which daily seek to influence our decisions and outlook on life.

Sometimes, when these forces fail to affect our own behavior, they resort to more cunning strategies, such as attacking our family members and others close to us in order to invade the purity of our thoughts and distract us from our calling in Christ. In addition, generational curses may continue in families for decades due to territorial demonic influences that have staked their claims over groups of people.

This is why we must truly understand how to exercise our spiritual authority and power. The only way to stop these toxic cycles is to take authority over them through Christ and fight against them vigilantly through prayer and the Word of God. Regardless of what assaults you face, when you remain steadfast in your faith and use the spiritual knowledge and weapons God has provided for you, you can counteract the enemy's attacks against you and your family. When you are armed with a divine revelation of who you are in Christ Jesus, it becomes increasingly impossible for the forces of evil to prevail against you, even in the midst of turmoil and adversity.

Those who have developed a close relationship with God through Christ are rarely caught off guard by Satan's attacks. By the time an attack manifests, they have already prayed and sought the Lord, and God's angels are standing guard to protect them as their deliverance begins to unfold.

Regardless of the circumstance, Jesus assures us that we hold the power, through His name, to persevere in times of testing and to overcome every attack the devil strategically sets for our demise. It is our desire to equip you with knowledge concerning both Satan's domain and the powerful deliverance of God, through Jesus Christ, which He has made available to all who believe.

INTRODUCTION

BY MARY K. BAXTER

In my first book, *A Divine Revelation of Hell*, I revealed how the Lord showed me life-altering visions of hell and the reality of that hideous place. When Jesus took me on my journey into hell, He said, "The day will come when you can reveal the things that I show you." From that time until the present, I have continued to see visions of God's miraculous power in operation and what is taking place behind the scenes in the spirit realm. I have described a number of these visions in my previous books. God has commissioned me by His power to reveal these visions to the body of Christ. I am also to share these powerful encounters with those who do not know Jesus as Lord and Savior, so that they may receive Him in the excellence of His power.

The ministry of deliverance manifests through a variety of gifts that the Lord has given to the body of Christ. My particular gift is dreams and visions. Visions are God's way of allowing us to take a glimpse into the miraculous world of His omnipotent power. As I have shared my visions and revelations, God has used them to loosen the devil's chains, to cast down demonic strongholds, and to set many people free in salvation and deliverance.

A DIVINE ENCOUNTER

After revealing my dreams and visions in my first book, I began traveling extensively, sharing with others these amazing encounters and encouraging men and women to come to Jesus Christ. It was during these travels that God's divine destiny caused the paths of Bishop George Bloomer and myself to cross. Since that time, we have ministered together on many occasions by the power of God so that thousands have been delivered and set free from years of torment, bondage, and demonic strongholds.

I identify our meeting as a *divine* encounter because God, knowing the gifts of the Spirit He has endowed within us both, saw fit to bring together our gifts in ministry. For years, Bishop Bloomer has been noted for his boldness in delivering the Word of God without hesitation. As we minister together, the power of the ministry of binding and loosing in Jesus' name is shown to be a powerful reality. (See Matthew 16:19; 18:18.)

REVELATIONS FOR TODAY

People's urgent need for deliverance and for a clearer understanding of God's power is what led us to expose more of Satan's tactics and deeds of darkness in this book. *A Divine Revelation of Deliverance* will reveal a number of real-life encounters and visions—some from years ago, some more recent—that the Lord has released me to share now with people throughout the world. We explain the reality of the gates of hell upon the earth (see Matthew 16:18 KJV), which are avenues of demonic attack, and which are also used to transport lost souls to an eternity without God. Most importantly, we share how to overcome demonic attacks through our Deliverer, the Lord Jesus Christ. Our prayer is that many more who are oppressed by the enemy will experience spiritual freedom.

RECOGNIZING SATAN'S DEVICES

Many of the hardships you are experiencing may have been inflicted upon you by the enemy, who seeks to destroy your confession of faith. The revelations that I received from God will help you to become aware of the devices of Satan. With this knowledge, you can properly invoke the power of Jesus Christ to overcome the invisible or hidden traps that have kept you bound.

These traps come by way of Satan's demonic forces. Each demon has been assigned certain duties to fulfill on the face of the earth to promote the ungodly and tragic reign of the *"ruler of this world"* (see John 12:30; 14:30; 16:11)—the devil's kingdom on earth. We are not powerless against these attacks, but we must realize their presence in order to destroy their existence.

God has given us the free will to make our own decisions. Yet the devil seeks to use our minds, wills, emotions, and bodies against us for his own tainted glory. Your choices do not have to be steered by the manipulative influences of Satan's domain. Regardless of how you may struggle with fear, rage, lust, addictions, or pain, your will to call upon the name of the Lord still remains. He will give you an answer if you will wait upon Him, continue seeking Him diligently in prayer, rely on His Spirit, and take action according to His Word.

> God will give you an answer if you will wait upon Him.

Jesus promised that the gates of hell would not prevail over the church—over those who know God and have received Him as personal Lord and Savior. *"On this rock I will build My church, and the gates of Hades* [hell] *shall not prevail against it"* (Matthew 16:18). I have prayed against demonic strongholds, and I have witnessed, right before my very eyes, the miraculous hand of God to set people free. I have seen people healed of physical ailments and delivered from demonic possession and oppression.

Exposing Satan and the Sinful Nature

With all the authority and power God has made available to the body of Christ, there is no need for a believer to suffer from anything that is not according to God's will. This is why Bishop Bloomer and I thought it not only timely, but also imperative, to expose the lies that keep so many bound, while also uncovering God-ordained ways of escape from Satan's designs and the sinful nature.

God has given you the power to speak the Word of God against demonic forces, and they have no choice but to flee. (See James 4:7.) *"The Lord knows those who are His"* (2 Timothy 2:19). He has made a covenant with all who call upon the name of Jesus. Through this covenant, we have the authority to rebuke the enemy when we are attacked by his ungodly influences, and to be set free when we are taken captive by his schemes. God has also given us the resurrection power of Jesus to overcome our sinful nature, which wages war against the nature and Spirit of God within us.

Our prayer is that you will discover your doorway to deliverance and that the chains of darkness, which have been keeping you bound, will be loosed. As the enemy's hidden hindrances are revealed, and as the workings of the sinful nature are exposed, may you learn to walk in the freedom and liberty God has ordained for your life.

—Mary K. Baxter

INTRODUCTION

BY GEORGE G. BLOOMER

For years I have preached a message of deliverance, revealing to those who are oppressed their right to live in freedom by the power of God. I have slept in the jungles of Africa, preached in the bush of the Philippines, ministered in India, and seen Muslims and Hindus give their lives to Christ. I have been on rescue trips with the Red Cross and have seen things that could torment you for the rest of your life. I have seen unexplainable phenomena in Haiti, such as levitations and the dead walking in the marketplace three days after their funerals. I have seen faces become contorted and heard several voices come out of one person's mouth while his tongue was not even moving.

Now I realize that all my studying, all my travel, and all those horrific things I saw and experienced were for such a time as this. They have enabled me to contribute to the writing of this book, which explains to you how the power of God delivers those who are bound by Satan. As you read *A Divine Revelation of Deliverance,* you can discover how to be set free from the bondages and strongholds the enemy has been holding over you.

TAKING A SPIRITUAL STAND

Today, more than ever, there is an urgent need within the body of Christ for the people of God to remain cognizant of their ability to have dominion over the things which have kept them bound. No longer can we sit idly by as observers. We must now take a spiritual stand against the havoc that is fighting against God's people.

God commanded mankind to have dominion over everything on the face of the earth. (See Genesis 1:26–28.) He also gave believers authority over Satan, in Jesus' name. (See, for example, Luke 9:1.) In order to activate your rights as a child of God, however, you must understand and apply them through His Word. If you do not know your authority, you will not be able to invoke it when faced with life's adversities and trials.

It is my responsibility as a spiritual leader in the body of Christ to reveal the truth concerning both the insidious deception of the demonic realm and the magnificent truth of God's deliverance. Yet choosing deliverance remains a decision only you can make. You no longer have to tolerate ungodly influences in your life; rather, you can learn to take dominion over the evil forces that have been attempting to overpower you!

A REVELATION OF GATES AND KEYS

This message of dominion is vividly presented in an exchange between the Lord Jesus and His disciple Peter. Peter answered the question that Jesus posed to His disciples, *"Who do men say that I, the Son of Man, am?"* by responding, *"You are the Christ, the Son of the living God"* (Matthew 16:13, 16). Jesus told him this fact could only have been revealed to him by the Father. He then equipped Peter with a truth that would forever secure his spiritual stand in glory:

> *And I also say to you that you are Peter, and on this rock I will build My church, and the **gates of Hades** ["hell" KJV] shall not prevail against it. And I will give you **the keys of the kingdom of heaven**, and whatever you bind on earth will be bound in heaven, and whatever you loose on earth will be loosed in heaven.*
>
> (Matthew 16:18–19, emphasis added)

Peter received a divine revelation that there are gates of hell, and that Jesus would give him keys—concepts, ideas, authority, insight, foresight, and the power to bind and loose—for overcoming them. The implication here is that hell does not start in the abyss, but that there could possibly be gates, or portals, of hell upon the earth. Moreover, whatever we bind on earth and whatever we loose on earth is bound and loosed in heaven. What is done on the earth can directly affect the heavenly realm.

Perhaps you are thinking, *So, you're telling me, Bishop, that you believe that hell's gates are on earth?* Yes, I do. I believe this in two ways. Not only are there actual invisible gates of hell on the earth that transport lost souls to hell, but there are also sensory "gates" in our lives that the devil uses in his schemes against us. In other words, he uses our senses—sight, hearing, touch, smell, and taste—to tempt our sinful natures and manipulate our minds by redirecting our desires and decisions away from God's will. When we give in to temptation and allow Satan to manipulate our minds, we may become involved in sinful and destructive practices, including sexual immorality, greed, pride, rage, addictions, and the occult.

> The devil uses our sight, hearing, touch, smell, and taste to tempt us.

Because of the attacks of the enemy, and the sinful nature that wars against the Spirit of God within us, the Scriptures tell us how we should think and what we should be thinking about:

Let this mind be in you which was also in Christ Jesus. (Philippians 2:5)

Finally, brethren, whatever things are true, whatever things are noble, whatever things are just, whatever things are pure, whatever things are lovely, whatever things are of good report, if there is any virtue and if there is anything praiseworthy; meditate on these things. (Philippians 4:8)

AUTHORITY OVER THE POWER OF THE ENEMY

Jesus understands our temptations as human beings, for He was tempted when He was on earth, though He never sinned. *"For we do not have a High Priest who cannot sympathize with our weaknesses, but was in all points tempted as we are, yet without sin"* (Hebrews 4:15). Jesus also knows what it is like to experience the direct attack of the enemy, and to overcome him. (See, for example, Matthew 4:1–11; Luke 22:39–42.)

Whether the devil uses our sinful nature against us through temptation or attacks us directly, we need to hold fast continually to the profession of our faith. When we do this, the strength and power of Jesus will save and deliver us from *all* the power of the enemy. Jesus said,

> *I saw Satan fall like lightning from heaven. Behold, I give you the authority to trample on serpents and scorpions, and **over all the power of the enemy,** and nothing shall by any means hurt you. Nevertheless do not rejoice in this, that the spirits are subject to you, but rather rejoice because your names are written in heaven.*
>
> (Luke 10:18–20, emphasis added)

—George G. Bloomer

1

ATTACKED BY THE GATES OF HELL

AN INCREASE IN DEMONIC ACTIVITY

I t was the mid-1970s when Jesus first revealed to me the horrors of hell, the tactics Satan uses in his attempts to destroy humanity, and how people need to be delivered from these attacks. Jesus warned me that Satan's assaults on the earth would increase as he released more demons from hell to cause rebellion and destruction.

Today, we are seeing the effects of these increased attacks on our world. There is more sin, and there have been more disasters, than ever before. We have had hurricanes, floods, tsunamis, and wars. (See Matthew 24:6–8.) Many people are facing intense spiritual attacks in their own lives and in the lives of their family members.

For Such a Time as This

I recently read over some of the prophecies that I have been writing down over the years, and I was in awe when I realized that many of these prophecies had come to pass without my even realizing it. I thought of how, in the 1980s, the Spirit of the Lord began to lead and guide me into all truth. (See John 16:13.) As I reflected, I sought God diligently, and I began to understand the purpose of my recording all the notes I had written throughout the years. God was preparing me then for what I am doing today. He was preparing me to share divine revelations with people and to assure them that they hold the power, through Christ Jesus, to stand tall and overcome the persistent obstacles that are holding them back in life. God wants us to put mere "religious" thinking under our feet and instead to build a secure relationship with Christ Jesus based on faith and trust in God—a relationship that will enable us to overcome all the assaults of the enemy.

With this book, I begin a journey of revealing some things I have not divulged in any of my other writings. It is by faith that I am able to share these visions God has shown to me. These are facts and truths that have been held back until such a time as this because the world could not receive them many years ago. I want to share with you from my heart what God has so graciously shared with me. It's very important to understand the hour in which we are living so that the will of God can be manifested in our lives.

POWER OVER HELL'S GATES

Two weeks before Christmas 2006, the Lord told me He wanted me to go on a fast, explaining that it would be very profitable for me. I was home alone and had time to pray, study and mediate on the Word, and seek the Lord. This opportunity excited me because I love God's Word. I believed that God would do what He said He was going to do during this time. (See Psalm 1:1–3.)

> **It is important to understand the times so the will of God can be manifested.**

Sometimes, when you are in the midst of spiritual warfare through fasting and prayer, you pray continuously. You get little sleep, and you are totally on your face before the Lord. You are travailing because God wants the Holy Spirit to move through you. You yield yourself to God completely, saying, "Here I am, God. Use me." As you submit yourself to Him through prayer, the Lord exposes revelation to you that can only be made known through the spirit realm.

A few days before Christmas, therefore, as I was really praying and seeking the Lord, I found myself being caught up in a vision. I saw the earth, and on it was a giant hole. I knew this was a gate of hell—which I will explain to you in more detail shortly—because God had been training me in the area of spiritual warfare. Out of this hole came hundreds of huge figures that were about twelve feet tall and looked like transparent penguins. As I was praying to the Lord, He said, "Call upon Me in the day of trouble, and I will deliver you." I began to say, "God, in the name of Jesus, I don't understand this, but I will call upon You to deliver us from whatever these things are."

I saw the hand of God come down, and I noticed the enormity of its size—it was about half as large as the earth. Out of His fingers came streams of fire. The flames shot into the large hole where these hideous, penguin-like figures were coming out at the surface of the earth, and cremated them. We read in Malachi,

> *"You shall trample the wicked, for they shall be ashes under the soles of your feet on the day that I do this," says the LORD of hosts.*   (Malachi 4:3)

The ashes of these figures began to blow away in the wind, and the Lord said, "I am destroying these evil powers." I watched as He burned millions of them. I concluded that this was God stopping some kind of attack of the enemy on us in regard to outbreaks of disease and other demonic activities. This is not to say that these figures always symbolize sickness, but that is what I discerned from this particular vision.

Later that day, I received a phone call from a prophet. As I began sharing with her what I had seen in the vision, she informed me that there had been a warning about bird flu. I began to praise the Lord for His deliverance because I knew that God had answered my request and given me my heart's desire. I have learned to obey God and to shut a gate of hell whenever He reveals it to me in a vision.

As I continued praying, I asked the Lord to bind this gate. I saw the earth shake, and I witnessed the hand of the Lord place a large cover, which looked as if it was made of iron, on the hole. Then I saw large angels swoop down with keys and chains and lock that gateway to hell. I began rejoicing in the Lord, saying, "Thank You, Jesus! You love us so much. Honor and majesty belong unto You, Lord. I put my trust in You!"

Jesus Is Our Deliverer

This incident illustrates just one of Satan's attacks against humanity in the last days. The gates of hell are assailing us, but Jesus can deliver you and your loved ones. We must know what we are battling and who is our Deliverer, so that we can fight effectively against these forces of evil. Many people on earth are being deceived and may fall into the schemes of Satan, or the devil, if we do not tell them of salvation and deliverance through Christ. We must return to the truth of Christ's death for us on the cross and our need for redemption through His sacrifice.

Satan desires to destroy every person on earth in whatever way he can. Yet the mercy of the Most High God has provided deliverance for you and me from the spiritual forces that attack us. Although we live in a day of great trouble and spiritual deception, we also have a great Deliverer, who has promised, *"Call upon Me in the day of trouble; I will deliver you, and you shall glorify Me"* (Psalm 50:15).

> **The mercy of God has provided deliverance for you.**

The devil uses a variety of schemes and methods to keep people from coming to know and love God, and to prevent those who do know and love Him from living productively for Him. He may attack us directly, or he may try to provoke our sinful human nature to do the work for him. I am very concerned because I see people falling into the enemy's traps, out of ignorance, and failing to find salvation through Christ. I also see Christians becoming discouraged, losing hope, and forsaking their faith because of the tests, temptations, and trials they experience. This alarms me because I have seen the cruel hatred the enemy has for humanity, and I have seen the fate of those who die without the Lord. I therefore urge you to learn and apply the deliverance God has provided for you. Jesus said,

> *I am He who lives, and was dead, and behold, I am alive forevermore. Amen. And I have the keys of Hades and of Death.*
> (Revelation 1:18)

Everything I am sharing with the body of Christ and with people at large through this book concerning the gates of hell is what God wants revealed to the world. Now is the time for these truths to be exposed to both Christians and non-Christians, to anyone who can grasp them and understand their significance.

A MESSAGE OF DELIVERANCE

God has a message of deliverance for us, and He has called me to give this message to the world.

During my travels, I was once in a foreign country to preach the gospel and an invitation came for me to have dinner with the wife of the president of that nation. I had set up a booking weeks prior to my arrival for another place about two hours away to preach a message on hell. After receiving this dinner invitation, however, I had to make a decision: either cancel my previously scheduled engagement or forgo the dinner invitation from the president's wife and send her a copy of the book instead. I decided to send the first lady an autographed copy of my book and continue with the previously scheduled engagement.

I went and preached to the people with love, and several souls were saved. I then returned to my room to retire for the night. Where I was staying, everyone always locked their doors, and dogs were let out at night to protect the property and people's belongings due to the high rate of theft in the area. They had dogs that guarded everything. I was really troubled because I had heard rumors approximately two weeks prior to my arrival about people carrying bombs into the city. About midnight, I heard guns going off and I thought, *Oh, my God! War has broken out! I'm going to die over here where nobody knows me, and without my family.* "Lord, You have to help me!" I pleaded.

As I continued praying, I had peace in my heart that surpassed all human understanding. (See Philippians 4:6–7.) I could hear thousands of guns going off and still did not have a clue as to what was taking place. The dogs were out and were barking. I thought that if I stepped outside, they would bite me, so I remained shut up within the safety of my quarters. As I sat huddled inside my room, I kept thinking about all the rumors that had been brewing—that war was about to break out and bombs were going to go off—so I prepared to die. I placed towels over the windows so that no one could see inside. I turned off all the lights, and when I peeked out the window I

> God has called me to bring His message of deliverance to the world.

could see the flashes of guns being fired in the dark of the night. As I sat there and said my prayers, I looked at the clock, and it was close to one in the morning. *At any minute, they're going to break in and kill me,* I kept thinking. Then, I had peace in my heart.

All at once, in one corner of the room, a bright light appeared on the wall. It circled around and then stopped. *They shot a missile in here!* I thought.

The more frightened I became, the more the light seemed to burst into a big flame, and then I saw what looked like a bush on fire. I realized, *This is what Moses saw—the burning bush!*

This bush was about five feet high and full of flames. I went over to it, put my hand in the fire, and felt a leaf. It looked like an oak leaf, and it was approximately half an inch thick of solid gold. I thought, *How beautiful.* I was in such shock that I forgot about the guns while looking at this tree. I began to worship and praise the Lord. Looking down at my feet, I said, "God, I've got my shoes off. You told Moses to take his shoes off because he was on holy ground, and Lord, I'm right here to listen to You." (See Exodus 3:2–5.)

I continued looking at this bush and telling God all my problems. All at once, everything became very quiet, and suddenly power came from the tree straight at me, and I fell backward. I remember crawling and forcing myself up so I could get into the bed. I looked back at the bush and prayed in my heart, *Dear God, what can I do for You?* I got back out of bed, pushed myself against this force, and stood in front of the bush again and tried to talk to God with all my heart, mind, and voice. The effect of this whole experience scared me so badly that I jumped into bed, pulled the covers over my head, and fainted!

The next morning, the birds were chirping, the dogs were still barking, the guns were still going off, and I realized, *I'm still alive*. I heard the men come to get the dogs and lock them up. Jumping out of bed, I screamed, "What is going on...and why all the guns? Has war broken out?"

A gentleman burst into laughter.

"Why are you laughing?" I asked.

"It's Mother's Day," he explained, "and here in this country we shoot the guns from midnight until noon to celebrate the mothers for the birth of the children."

I thought, *Why didn't someone tell me!*

As the people tried to comfort me, the guns were still going off, and I remained very upset. A few minutes later, I heard a truck pull up out front, and the person who had been my interpreter came in and said that she had a message for me from the Lord. "As I was doing my dishes, the Lord spoke to me," she began to share. "He told me to give you a message, and here it is. He told me to first ask you, 'Did He appear to you last night?'"

I was still so scared that I answered, "Maybe... sort of...kind of...yes, He did."

Then she said, "You fainted, right?"

"Yes...I did."

"The message is this: God has given unto you the keys to the kingdom, and as He was with Moses, He shall be with you. You are His deliverer in this hour to deliver people from the devil's hand, as Moses delivered the people of his day from the hands of Pharaoh. You are His deliverer, and you are to take these messages all over the earth to set the people free from the devil's hand. You are to do what the Lord has called you to do and to fear no man. He wants you to be encouraged and go tell these stories in other lands and countries."

> God used my circumstances to give me guidance about my life and ministry.

Although my concern about the guns had been a misunderstanding, God used this circumstance to give me guidance about my life and ministry. He showed me that He would be with me and that I was not to be afraid of what others might say or do. I began to cry and praise the Lord. I thanked the interpreter for the message, and she was so glad that she had obeyed the voice of the Lord and told me these things. I continued to praise God and to hang on to His promise.

I have experienced many things, such as this one, that I have never before told anyone. Yet now is the time for me to share even more of my miraculous and supernatural experiences. I tell these stories in obedience and according to the leading of the Holy Spirit. We must truly know that God is more than able to deliver, according to His Word.

AN ARMY STRONG AND UNAFRAID

We are living in a time when many more demons have come out of the gates of hell and into the earth's atmosphere to cause widespread deception. Yet, in the midst of it all, God has an army of His people that is fighting for the truth—an army that is standing tall and preaching holiness and righteousness to rescue individuals and families.

With this book, I hope to add to this army of believers that is not afraid of the devil but understands Satan is fighting a losing battle. Jesus holds the keys to death and hell. He knows every trick the devil tries to use for our demise, and He gives us instructions on how to counteract these evil attacks. As we learn Satan's tactics, we must always remember that Jesus has the power to overcome anything that may come against us and anything that we may face, and that we can have complete victory over the enemy.

There are great tribulations in the earth, but God Almighty wants to lock the gates of hell, and He wants you to join in the battle against the enemy.

2

DEMONIC DECEPTION

In this chapter, I will describe in more detail some of the assaults that are coming against us in our nation and around the world, as well as the depth of the deception and torment Satan seeks to inflict upon us. We will see how much we need our Deliverer, who gives us the authority to overcome all the power of the enemy.

THE WORLD IS BEING DECEIVED

Desensitized to the Dangers of the Demonic

There are three main ways in which the enemy is deceiving the world today. First, among people who are seeking a "higher power" for answers to life's crises, there is a growing curiosity about mysticism, Eastern religions, and the occult. Through these avenues, many are unknowingly being lured into the demonic realm of Satan's domain. Television and other media have romanticized magic and the demonic to the point that it is no longer considered taboo for a person to dabble in the world of the occult; it has become a fad. People do not realize these things are detrimental to their spiritual well-being. Society has become desensitized to the dangers of embracing the demonic realm, and people are increasingly opening their homes and hearts to satanic and ungodly influences.

The devil takes advantage of any opportunity that presents itself to inject false doctrines into the minds of those who are in spiritual pursuit of a higher power and peace. This is how people often wind up in cults and occult worship, for example, or engulfed in demoralizing behavior. Many of their relatives and friends are bewildered about how their loved ones could ever have become deceived by such obvious religious fallacies. The person being deceived has no idea that what he or she considers spiritual "completion" is actually a ploy from the devil to promote false doctrine and spiritual deception in his or her life, leading to destruction.

> We must proclaim the liberty people can have through Jesus Christ.

The apostle Paul warned against the dangers of worshipping false gods or anything that exalts itself above the knowledge of the true and living God. (See 2 Corinthians 10:4–5.) Yet the worship of false gods and idols continues to run rampant in our world. Those who know God and His Son Jesus Christ must take a stand against the manipulation of the true gospel of salvation through Christ. False gospels are luring people away from God instead of bringing them into His presence.

We must take the initiative to help people understand what is happening to them as they are influenced by the unseen forces of evil principalities and powers that seek to destroy them. We must proclaim the liberty they can have in the Lord Jesus Christ. If we don't, not only will they remain captives of the enemy on this earth, but they will also experience a horrible hell in eternity. We must warn people of God's judgment before it is too late.

We cannot take lightly the significance of what Jesus accomplished on the cross in order to save the world from this destruction. The gospel of the Lord Jesus Christ must be proclaimed in order to set people free.

Lacking a Reverence for God

Second, multitudes of people are dying and going to hell because they have no reverence for

God or don't acknowledge His existence. More and more, the devil is attempting to portray God as a fictional character rather than allowing people to see Him for who He really is—the Creator and Sustainer of our lives. The Scriptures tell us, *"For in [God] we live and move and have our being"* (Acts 17:28). At the same time, Satan is trying to hide the reality of hell so that it appears as science fiction concocted in the imagination of creative storytellers, rather than the hideous place it truly is.

I really believe that if people had a reverence for God, they would become much more cognizant of their actions and realize the priceless gift of eternal life offered through Jesus Christ. No longer would they continue to bow to the beckoning of demonic voices.

Confused and Living in Immorality

Third, Satan is camouflaging and watering down the gospel of Jesus Christ in order to seduce people through sensuality and addictions. The youth of our day have especially seen much corruption. Their minds have been so polluted by ungodliness disguised as morality that they find it difficult to discern God's truth from deception. The devil preys upon their vulnerabilities, luring them into a world of idolatry and deceit that undermines their spiritual well-being and can lead to complete self-destruction. He manipulates youthful naiveté to promote his false doctrine through peer pressure and by romanticizing toxic behavior. More and more, the depraved content of many television programs reveals the work of demons that have been released to influence those who have lost their fear of God. Nothing seems off-limits, and people are more prone to act upon whatever lust or perversion appeases the fleshly nature.

This cultural attitude has opened our homes to moral turpitude beyond comprehension, with wickedness being viewed as a normal lifestyle rather than as a pathway to degradation and destruction. For example, a young Christian man met a beautiful girl in college. As the relationship began to flourish, she asked him, "Will you come to my home and meet my parents?" He agreed to do so, but when he arrived at her home, he became very dismayed. He saw two women, and inquired of his companion, "Where is your father?" to which she replied, "This woman is my father, and my mother's husband." The young man was so upset that

> **Wickedness is viewed as normal rather than a pathway to destruction.**

he went home and wept before the Lord, "What can I do, God? What can I say to help people?"

The challenges that our youth face today are even more demanding and overt than those of previous generations; these challenges cling to them like a glove, and they need the freedom that can only come through Christ.

GATEWAYS OR PORTALS TO HELL

We must truly understand the underlying demonic causes that are behind many of the personal and societal troubles we are currently facing. At the same time, we must be assured that there is complete victory in Jesus Christ. In some of my previous books, I have described how Christ appeared to me and showed me, through visions and revelations, the depths of hell and the peace and joy of heaven. He took me on a journey for three hours each night for thirty nights to the very bowels of the earth to show me the judgment of His Father upon rebellion and sin.

He also showed me visions of the "gateways to hell," which are the sources of many of our demonic attacks today. These experiences were so incredibly real that I could reach out and touch the images as He revealed them to me. He led me to what first appeared to be a whirlwind of powders mixed with different lights and colors of brown and white. Upon further investigation, however, I noticed that this tornado-like image was not moving. It was still, and it was hooked onto the earth. There were several of these circular figures; some of them were transparent, while the others were opaque, and they swung back and forth very slowly. These gates of hell came out of the earth and extended high into the galaxy.

Jesus explained, "These are the gates of hell. I'm going to take you down one of these gates and into hell." As we descended into this gate, Christ reminded me that in His hand was a ring of keys. The keys were the keys of death and hell that He took from the devil. In Revelation 1:17–18, Jesus said, *"I am the First and the Last. I am He who lives, and was dead, and behold, I am alive forevermore. Amen. And I have the keys of Hades and of Death."* We do not have to fear Satan because Jesus has already gained the victory over him.

> We do not have to fear Satan because Jesus has already gained the victory.

Around the inside of this gate of hell, which looked like a tunnel, there was a transparent gray mesh. Behind the mesh were many demons or devils. Some of them were clinging to the wall, while others were climbing about and screaming at me. Doors were at the top of the tunnel.

Among the demons I encountered in this gate, some were about twelve feet tall and appeared as silhouettes of cockroach-like figures. There were also demonic figures in the form of enormous spiders that crawled around and looked extraordinarily sinister. Other creatures had faces that were about two feet wide, with very long, pointed noses, and fangs; they had tails with a fork at the end, and wings that allowed them to fly. They had hooves, with sharp, razor-like claws that could tear you to shreds. Worms crawled about in their wings, and they were some of the most gruesomely demonic figures I have ever seen. In this gate of hell there was also a horrendous odor of demonic sulfur mixed with the smell of mud and the worst odor of burning flesh.

As we went down this gateway, Christ told me the day would come when all these evil beings would be released upon the earth to do the devil's bidding. It has been a long time since Jesus showed me hell, but as I wrote earlier, in the past few years, more sin has abounded. These hideous spirits have now come out of hell and attacked the masses.

THE REALITY OF HELL

The reality of Satan, demons, and hell is written about in the Scriptures. Jesus said there is an *"everlasting fire prepared for the devil and his angels"* (Matthew 25:41). Hell was prepared for the devil and the angels who followed him in his rebellion against God. Yet, since Satan also enticed human beings to rebel and follow him, people who do not love and serve God—who continue to be self-indulgent, following their own ways and rejecting God's commandments and forgiveness through Christ—will end up there, too. (See Matthew 25:14–46.)

The Scriptures refer to following our own way, rather than God's, as doing the *"works of the flesh."*

> *Now the works of the flesh are evident, which are: adultery, fornication, uncleanness, lewdness, idolatry, sorcery, hatred, contentions, jealousies, outbursts of wrath, selfish ambitions, dissensions, heresies, envy, murders, drunkenness, revelries, and the like; of which I tell you beforehand, just as I also told you in time past, that those who practice such things will not inherit the kingdom of God.*
>
> (Galatians 5:19–21)

Again, hell was not made for people, especially God's people. (Please be assured that babies do not go to hell, nor do young children. Jesus is merciful, and God continues to protect the innocent.) Yet because of humanity's rebellion and sin against the Creator, hell has enlarged itself and made room to hold people's souls. (See Isaiah 5:11–15.) Many who mocked the Lord Jesus Christ instead of embracing Him while they were alive on the earth now reside in hell. Others are there who committed hideous offenses and never repented.

> **Hell was not made for people—especially God's people.**

Jesus made these statements, among others, about the reality of hell:

> *Do not fear those who kill the body but cannot kill the soul. But rather fear Him who is able to destroy both soul and body in hell.* (Matthew 10:28)

> *And you, Capernaum, who are exalted to heaven, will be brought down to Hades; for if the mighty works which were done in you had been done in Sodom, it would have remained until this day. But I say to you that it shall be more tolerable for*

*the land of Sodom in the day of judgment
than for you.* (Matthew 11:23–24)

Hell's reality is inexplicable. When I witnessed it in my visions, all I could feel was fear and death all around me. Thank God that Jesus was with me and consoled me to "fear not." He reminded me that I would share these visions with people throughout the world, and because of it, many souls would be saved.

THE COST OF REJECTING JESUS

No More Opportunities to Repent

I have spoken to others who have encountered gateways to hell, and I remember their descriptions of how it felt as they descended into the tunnel. They actually felt as if the evil spirits were trying to reach out and grab them. These same spirits would boldly articulate threats, such as "We've got you now," "It's too late," "We deceived you," "You could've had Jesus!"

When you reject Jesus, you invite into your life the toxicity of ungodliness and a future of torment. It's the most hideous thing to walk among the dead in hell. The souls there are very cognizant of the fact that life is continuing on the earth and that they had every chance to repent before they were doomed to this awful, eternal place. I can still remember the screams of the dead echoing in the darkness, along with their cries of repentance—their regret and the realization that they were burning in hell. My heart broke for them, and I cried out, "Lord, how can I help them? What can I tell them?" I thought of the people's ignorance concerning the judgment of God, and I began to think clearly of this journey through hell and of the need to be very specific and precise in what God was showing me so that I could better relay this truth to the world.

Punishment of Fire

When people on the earth have rejected the gospel and die without Jesus, demons seize them, put a chain around them, and drag them down a gateway into hell. There, they are thrown off a cliff into a valley of fire and are held in a holding place. Many souls are thrown into this valley of fire before being thrust into their places of judgment within the different compartments of hell.

The compartments of hell have varying degrees of fire—some hotter than others. Each compartment represents certain laws of God that have been broken. If you are a murderer, you are placed in a compartment with all the murderers; if you are a liar, you are put with all the liars, and so forth. The souls in these compartments had served their fleshly nature rather than God, and had not chosen to repent.

Fear and Loss

As I traveled with Jesus down the gateway to hell, fear came upon me, and I felt as if everything within me and everything precious to me had departed—my love, my home, my family. It was the most horrible feeling you can ever imagine.

THE NEED FOR HOLINESS

As we progressed down the gateway, great snakes, large rats, and many evil spirits ran from the presence of the Lord. When we entered one place, the snakes hissed at us, and the rats squeaked; they made evil sounds. Large vipers and dark shadows were all about us. Jesus was the only light, and I stayed close to Him. Imps and devils were all along the side of this tunnel. I knew these evil beings had the ability to become invisible to the natural eye because I had seen them going upon the earth to do Satan's bidding. Feeling my fear of this dark, dirty place, Jesus said, "Fear not. We will be at the end of this soon. I must show you many things. Come, follow Me."

Snakes slid past us, and dirty smells were everywhere. The snakes there were very fat and round—about four feet around and twenty-five feet long. I saw black muck, and it seemed to billow up and down. An odor of dung was in the air and evil spirits were everywhere. Fear filled the air, and I knew there was still much ahead that I had to see, but Jesus gave me peace. He told me, "We'll soon be at the center of hell."

The center of hell appeared to be more than fifteen miles high, and the belly of hell looked approximately three miles in circumference. I remembered Jesus' words—that He was showing me all these things to tell the world that they are real.

> If we fail, the Lord will pick us up if we repent.

There is a section in hell for the souls who have done great wickedness against the Lord and His people. Sorcerers, evil women and men who would not repent, are in jail cells. Evil and sin are their gods. I heard the Lord say to me, "Be ye holy, for I am holy. Do good and repent in My name. I am the Door. If you are faithful and true, come and follow Me." (See 1 Peter 1:16; John 10:7–9; Matthew 19:21.) I made up my mind to walk clean before the Lord. I knew that even if I failed, He would be right there to pick me up if I repented, because I belonged to Him.

Demonic Forces Released from Hell

While hell is a place of punishment for those who reject God, it is also a place from which evil spirits come to attack us. When Jesus took me into hell, He explained that, at certain times, Satan gives orders, and demonic spirits are released into the atmosphere to go into the earth and other places. Today, many gates of hell emerge from the middle of the earth. Demonic powers are sent upon the earth to do bidding for the devil.

These things, you can be assured, are very real. We are fighting spiritual battles, just as we read about in the book of Daniel. (See Daniel 10.) I remember so well seeing the warfare that takes place in the heavenly realm against seducing spirits that come against us. I pleaded, "Oh, God, please help us not to fall into the hands of these seducing powers and into these evil ways." It broke my heart to see this evil leader sending demonic forces upon the earth to spread his deception.

Engaged in a Fierce Spiritual War

Although demonic power is hideous and strong, Jesus is stronger, and He is our Deliverer. Jesus told me that the gates of hell will *not* prevail against the church. (See Matthew 16:18.) That is why it is so important that I relay this message of deliverance to everyone. We must learn to trust Jesus fully as Deliverer and to bind demonic forces while loosing the blessings of God in the name of Jesus.

We are engaged in a spiritual battle that must be fought with the supernatural armament of God, through His power. God alone can give us victory over Satan, the *"prince of the power of the air"* (Ephesians 2:2), and the rulers of demon darkness and spiritual wickedness in the heavenly places. Ephesians 6:11–12 admonishes us,

> *Put on the whole armor of God, that you may be able to stand against the wiles of the devil. For we do not wrestle against flesh and blood, but against principalities, against powers, against the rulers of the darkness of this age, against spiritual hosts of wickedness in the heavenly places.*

We are to engage in spiritual warfare not only for our own sakes, but also for the sake of multitudes of people who are being ensnared by the devil. In Matthew 18:21, Peter asked how many times he should forgive the offense of his brother, and Jesus replied, *"I do not say to you, up to seven times, but up to seventy times seven"* (v. 22). Forgiveness is the nature of God. He is a God of mercy and grace. He admonishes us to offer the same love to others as He bestows upon us. We must restore those who have fallen away from God and bring into His kingdom those who do not yet know Him. We must help to free people from the attacks and control of Satan.

It bothers me greatly to think of the many people who are going to hell because they do not have a healthy fear of God and are not saved. As we have seen, people today openly invite hell into their lives by embracing ungodly, demonic behavior. The demons oppress or possess them and use them as vessels to carry out their evil acts. When I was with Jesus in hell, I thought, *These gates of hell need to be bound shut because the enemy is spewing all kinds of evil forces into the earth, such as pornography and the destruction of marriages, homes, and children.*

> We must help free people from the attacks and control of Satan.

I wrote this book as a tool to expose the deeds of darkness, reveal their origin, and give those who are bound the hope of knowing they can be set free by the power of God. Hideous things come out of hell when Satan gives orders for them to go upon the earth. Evil spirits are walking about, seeking whom they may devour (see 1 Peter 5:8), and people are yielding themselves to these ungodly powers. Yet God is warning people to stop the evil they are doing and to turn to the Lord Jesus Christ before it is too late.

You may use whatever philosophy you like to tone down the reality and danger of ungodly acts, but the truth remains the same. We must take hold of reality, giving no more loyalty to groups of people who want to make excuses for living a life of demoralization and ungodliness. In the Bible, the Lord rained down fire on Sodom and Gomorrah because of their utter rejection of His ways, and the Scriptures tell us that a final judgment day will come upon all people of the earth. (See, for example, 1 Peter 4:5; Revelation 20:11–15.) Jesus promised, *"The sign of the Son of Man will appear in the sky, and all the nations of the earth will mourn. They will see the Son of Man coming on the clouds of the sky, with power and great glory"* (Matthew 24:30). We have to watch for Jesus, believing that He's coming back and will judge the world. *"The Lord Jesus Christ...will judge the living and the dead at His appearing and His kingdom"* (2 Timothy 4:1).

DESTRUCTIVE DOCTRINES OF DEMONS

Make no mistake about it: We are in a war of good versus evil. This is a crucial war for multitudes of souls. We are battling doctrines of demons that have come into our land to deceive the people.

Now the Spirit expressly says that in latter times some will depart from the faith, giving heed to deceiving spirits and doctrines of demons, speaking lies in hypocrisy, having their own conscience seared with a hot iron. (1 Timothy 4:1–2)

These doctrines teach lies and hypocrisy. They tell us not to believe the Word of the Lord and try to belittle the truth and power that reign from heaven. They tell you that you can behave anyway you want because God lives in you and He "understands." These false doctrines imply that God will simply look the other way and accept teachings that contradict His Word. Some even say there is no God at all.

For false christs and false prophets will rise and show great signs and wonders to deceive, if possible, even the elect.
(Matthew 24:24)

Those who promote false doctrines sometimes back up their claims with counterfeit signs and wonders, which do not come from God. These are seducing spirits that are manifesting in order to promote their demonic propaganda.

There is a time and a place where you need to hear the truth and be set free. That time and place is now. Learn the truth of the gospel, not only for your own sake, but also for the sake of others who are suffering under doctrines of demons and need God's deliverance. Fight the devil and know that you have power over him in the name of Jesus. We have to believe that Jesus is Lord and that His mercy will reach out to those who are being deceived. While Satan comes to kill, steal, and destroy, Jesus comes to give us life, and to give it more abundantly. (See John 10:10.)

> While Satan comes to steal, kill, and destroy, Jesus comes to give us life.

EXTINGUISHING DOUBT AND UNBELIEF

Throughout the Word of God, the Lord extinguishes doubt and unbelief while showing forth His great power. He will do the same for us today. In 1 Kings 18, we read how God sent His prophet Elijah to expose the powerless god Baal. Elijah said to the people of Israel, who were worshipping this false god,

> *"Then you call on the name of your gods, and I will call on the name of the LORD; and the God who answers by fire, He is God."*

So all the people answered and said, "It is well spoken." Now Elijah said to the prophets of Baal, "Choose one bull for yourselves and prepare it first, for you are many; and call on the name of your god, but put no fire under it." (1 Kings 18:24–25)

In vain, the followers of Baal called upon their god. Yet, when Elijah called upon the name of the Lord over His sacrifice, there was no question as to who was and remains the true and living God: *"Then the fire of the LORD fell and consumed the burnt sacrifice, and the wood and the stones and the dust, and it licked up the water that was in the trench"* (v. 38).

Just as God defeated Baal, He continues to defeat false gods and doctrines of demons today. The Word of God and His power are extraordinary and too remarkable for our natural minds to comprehend. You can accept this truth or reject it, but I admonish you to hear and receive the Word of the Lord. God's Word means what it says and performs what it promises. We must remove our doubt and unbelief, stand in the office of God's Word, speak His Word, and remind the devil that he is defeated by the blood of the Lamb.

God's Word is greater than any attack the enemy tries to conjure up for our demise. This is why we must let go of moaning and complaining and being fearful—our frequent reaction to trouble—and arm ourselves with the weaponry God has given us as we fight the good fight of faith!

> *Those who desire to be rich* [including any of the world's false riches and promises] *fall into temptation and a snare, and into many foolish and harmful lusts which drown men in destruction and perdition. For the love of money is a root of all kinds of evil, for which some have strayed from the faith in their greediness, and pierced themselves through with many sorrows. But you, O man of God, flee these things and pursue righteousness, godliness, faith, love, patience, gentleness.* **Fight the good fight of faith,** *lay hold on eternal life, to which you were also called and have confessed the good confession in the presence of many witnesses.*
>
> (1 Timothy 6:9–12, emphasis added)

3

Whom Will You Serve?

I n these times of increased spiritual warfare, we are being called to make a decision. Just as the people of Israel had to make a clear decision between the living God and the false god Baal, each of us has to make a clear decision between God's kingdom of light and the devil's kingdom of darkness. Will we serve God, or will we serve Satan—either through outright allegiance to the enemy, or through succumbing to his lies and the enticements of the flesh and forfeiting our relationship with God?

The Lord often reveals to me His desire to see spiritual captives set free. God does not want anyone to go to hell. This is why He has commissioned me to share the deep revelations He has shown me in the Spirit and why I am so candid about urging people to turn back to God.

We must comprehend the nature and implications of our choice: we are choosing between the ferociousness of hell and its opposite—the love of God. God desires to keep us close in His care. He is not a vicious dictator, hovering over us and waiting for us to sin so He can cast us into the lake of fire. He tells us in His Word that He did not send Jesus to condemn the world but to redeem it. *"God did not send His Son into the world to condemn the world, but that the world through Him might be saved"* (John 3:17). His desire is that we will embrace the gift of eternal life by repentance through Christ, and that we will continue to follow Him all the days of our lives.

> **God loves us so much that He allows us to choose to accept His love.**

To whom will *you* give your allegiance—a loving God or a hateful devil? Where will you spend eternity—living an abundant life with your loving Creator or suffering terrible punishment along with His enemy? God loves and respects us so much that He does not force Himself or His gifts upon us. He allows us to make the decision.

In the book of Joshua, the second generation of Israelites was also admonished to make this significant decision. By the same decree that He spoke through Joshua to the Israelites, the Lord poses to us our option: *"choose for yourselves this*

day whom you will serve" (Joshua 24:15). The
Word of God is clear:

> *No man can serve two masters: for either
> he will hate the one, and love the other; or
> else he will hold to the one, and despise
> the other.*   (Matthew 6:24)

Whom are you currently serving? What is
your "god"? Is it money, sex, addiction, your job,
or even your family? Whatever is capable of oc-
cupying your attention and loyalty more than
God ultimately becomes your god. Satan then
uses these things to keep you from hearing the
Word of the Lord and to steer you further into the
depths of darkness. The devil knows that if he can
clog your mind with the cares of this world, then
you are less able to discern spiritual matters and
more inclined to give in to the constant tug of the
fleshly nature. This is why the Word of the Lord
instructs us concerning what to keep our minds
focused on at all times:

> *Finally, brethren, whatever things are true,
> whatever things are noble, whatever things
> are just, whatever things are pure, what-
> ever things are lovely, whatever things are
> of good report, if there is any virtue and if
> there is anything praiseworthy; meditate
> on these things.*   (Philippians 4:8)

CONSEQUENCES OF THE FALL OF HUMANITY

Imagine, for a moment, that you are living in complete utopia in the garden of Eden, just as the first man and woman on earth experienced. Your thirst is quenched by pure water drawn from Eden's river. Your hunger is satisfied by food grown in the garden of God as you picnic beneath shade trees strategically placed as nature's shield from the sun. Meanwhile, you are serenaded by the melodious tunes of the heavenly host. This band scripts its lyrics from God's Word, and its tunes throb directly from God's heart. You have a sense of complete purpose and fulfillment as you carry out God's work in the world He created especially for human beings, who are made in His image.

> We are made in God's image, and our purpose is to carry out His work in the world.

When we compare this scenario with the strife of the world today, we see that humanity's rebellion and fall caused a tremendous loss to human beings. Yet God still paved a way to reconcile humanity to Himself. Consider the following Scriptures:

For God so loved the world that He gave His only begotten Son, that whoever

believes in Him should not perish but have
everlasting life. (John 3:16)

God was in Christ reconciling the world
to Himself, not imputing their trespasses
to them. (2 Corinthians 5:19)

While the devil deceived the first human beings, promoting their downfall (see Genesis 3),
and continues to deceive the human race, the
Lord has provided a way of escape for us. It was
never God's intention that we suffer by becoming disconnected from His presence. Although
sin separated us from Him, our repentance and
submission through Christ's sacrifice reconnect
us. When God becomes our Father through Jesus
Christ, we are the heirs of God, and He grants us
access to Himself and His kingdom.

For as many as are led by the Spirit of
God, these are sons of God. For you did
not receive the spirit of bondage again to
fear, but you received the Spirit of adop-
tion by whom we cry out, "Abba, Father."
The Spirit Himself bears witness with our
spirit that we are children of God, and
if children, then heirs; heirs of God and
joint heirs with Christ, if indeed we suffer
with Him, that we may also be glorified to-
gether....For the earnest expectation of the

creation eagerly waits for the revealing of the sons of God. (Romans 8:14–17, 19)

GOD'S NATURE VERSUS THE DEVIL'S NATURE

The love, forgiveness, and grace of God are in complete contrast to the utter evil of Satan. The enemy desires to deceive and torment people. When I was taken to hell and saw the many demons with their distorted faces, they were always mocking and speaking to the doomed souls, "You could have had Jesus, but we deceived you." Then they would laugh at the screams of the dead. Over and over, I would see these foul spirits tormenting souls. Some would put fire on them, while others would come to the edge of where they were locked in their various compartments and burn them even more. In one part of hell, I watched as, over and over, gigantic snakes slithered while fire protruded from their mouths in a frightening way.

I would also see the devil. Sometimes, he would make the demons look like humans and send them upon the earth. He would give them certain jobs to perform, and if they did not carry out their tasks, he would expose them to the people. This is the nature of the devil. He is true to nothing and no one, not even his vehicles of deception.

Though the truth concerning the hideousness of hell must be revealed, we must fully realize that this horrible place does not have to be our destination. Because of Christ's love for us, He died on the cross—taking the punishment we deserved. He took the keys of hell and the grave; He saved us and gave us the gift of eternal life with Him, so we would not have to experience torment.

WHOSE VOICE WILL YOU LISTEN TO?

In the garden of Eden, the ears of human beings were originally attuned to the voice of God. At the fall of man, however, Adam and Eve sought the knowledge of good and evil, presuming they could be equal with God; they became wise in their own sight, choosing to ignore the wisdom and omniscience of God. It was then that humanity's ears became attuned to the seductive enticements of the devil.

From the point of humanity's rejection of God, every human being has been born in sin and *"shaped in iniquity"* (Psalm 51:5 KJV). Have you ever wondered, for instance, why you never have to tell an infant or toddler how to misbehave? He automatically knows what to do to get into trouble. He has to be taught the proper actions in order to do what is pleasing to his father or mother. Likewise, we have to be taught that we have a Father who loves us and has our best interests at heart. At first, we may not always want to take the advice of our Father, but in the end we must realize that He knows what is right and that His intention is to lead us out of harm's way. God knows how to take care of those who belong to Him.

All human beings are sinners by nature, and sin births condemnation. The feelings of unworthiness that are associated with condemnation often prevent people from coming back to God for restoration. This sense of being condemned comes to people who are not Christians, but it can also come to Christians who fall, feel guilty, and don't believe they can be restored to God.

> God's grace gives us the opportunity to come to Him for wisdom and strength.

Yet, again, God is merciful and does not stand by waiting for us to sin so He can toss us away. His grace, poured out through His Spirit, gives us the opportunity to come to Him for forgiveness, wisdom, and strength.

We must listen to what God offers us and not be deceived by the lies of the enemy, who tells us we can never be forgiven and return to God. People who constantly operate according to their own wills, without ever consulting God about anything and without coming to Him in repentance, are some of the most dangerous people in the world.

WHAT ARE YOUR INWARD INTENTIONS?

God does not look on the outward appearance but judges us based upon the intentions of the heart. (See 1 Samuel 16:7.) We can hide our sins from other people, but we cannot hide them from God; neither can we hide from Him the true intentions of our hearts. He cannot be fooled.

There was a Buddhist monk in China who died and witnessed the treachery of hell. He testified how, although his body was dead for three days, his spirit was very much alert. In hell, the truth concerning the plight of those who worship idols and false gods, and who reject Jesus, was revealed to him. He was astonished to see many of the great teachers of old there, who had been condemned to hell because of their unbelief and false doctrines. The monk was allowed to come back to life, and when he awoke in his coffin—much to the astonishment of those attending his funeral—and gave his testimony, many still did not believe.

The gospel has been preached over and over again, but thousands continue to love their own personal lifestyles more than they love and reverence God. If they were to turn back to God and trust Him to protect them, they would see significant changes take place in their lives and in the lives of their loved ones.

God has given me a burden to reveal the love of Christ so that you may escape the snare of the enemy and be filled with the fullness of God. Today, you can possess the power of God in your life while experiencing peace, love, and joy in the Holy Spirit.

You Must Make a Choice

As I was crying out for souls one day and praying with a prophet, a vision of a valley appeared to me. There were mounds of dirt in certain places with hands emerging from them, and I heard screaming. As the hands appeared from out of the dirt, I saw blackness rolling off them and also from the hearts of these people. The Lord was speaking, "I want souls to be saved."

When I had the vision of hell, Jesus showed me the significance of repenting and turning back to Him. Now, more than ever, God is calling people back to Him to repent of their sins. His grace, through the blood of His Son, will wash you clean. His mercy is everlasting, and His love is reaching out to you today.

These are evil times when we especially need Jesus. I must do everything that I can to make this generation aware of the options concerning its eternal fate. The Lord told the Israelites, *"I call heaven and earth as witnesses today against you, that I have set before you life and death, blessing and cursing; therefore choose life, that both you and your descendants may live"* (Deuteronomy 30:19). Again, God does not force His love on us, but He sets before us two options: life or death, blessing or cursing. He allows us to make the choice for ourselves and does not force His will upon us. *"He who believes in Him is not condemned; but he who does not believe is condemned already, because he has not believed in the name of the only begotten Son of God"* (John 3:18). I admonish you to choose life so that the blessings of God will not only be upon you, but also upon your descendants.

> God sets before us two options: life or death, blessing or cursing.

Jesus shed His blood on the cross because He knew His destiny. He knew He would have the joy of saving multitudes of lost souls and providing eternal life for them. He knew He would rise from the dead and return to the Father in heaven to intercede for His people.

*Looking unto Jesus, the author and fin-
isher of our faith, who for the joy that was
set before Him endured the cross, despis-
ing the shame, and has sat down at the
right hand of the throne of God.*

(Hebrews 12:2)

*Therefore He is also able to save to the ut-
termost those who come to God through
Him, since He always lives to make intercession for them.* (Hebrews 7:25)

God loves you so much that He gave His only
Son to save you from eternal damnation. Please do
not take this lightly. This is the time that we must
turn back to God. We must learn of His eternal
grace and mercy and how He wants us to be clean
and pure through the blood of His Son and His
righteousness. Yes, you may fall at times; however, if you continue to seek the Lord earnestly
with a sincere heart to be led by Him in paths of
righteousness, you can get up again. If you continue to reach out to Jesus, you will begin to see
His perfect will, authority, and power manifested
in your life as never before.

*For a righteous man may **fall** seven times
and rise again, but the wicked shall fall
by calamity.*

(Proverbs 24:16, emphasis added)

You Can Be Saved

How do you receive salvation and remain in the power and protection of Christ? First, the Scriptures tell us,

> *If you **confess** with your mouth the Lord Jesus **and believe** in your heart that God has raised Him from the dead, you will be saved.* (Romans 10:9, emphasis added)

Salvation begins with a confession. Ultimately, what you believe in your heart will to come out of your mouth; therefore, what you confess reveals what is in your heart. What are you currently confessing over your life that is contrary to a confession of faith in Christ and is causing you to remain in a bad predicament? What beliefs do you have in your heart that keep you disconnected from God? Whatever these things are, get rid of them and believe the Word of God. Confess with your mouth that God raised Jesus from the dead; believe this in your heart, and you will be saved.

> *For with the heart one believes unto righteousness, and with the mouth confession is made unto salvation.* (Romans 10:10)

You cannot confess with your mouth until you first believe in the Lord Jesus Christ in your heart. This is why salvation can never be forced on anyone. It is an act of *voluntarily, willingly* surrendering your will to the will and purpose of God.

Whatever lies in your heart shapes your beliefs. This means that the more you receive the Word of God into your heart, the more your faith can be built. *"Faith comes by hearing, and hearing by the word of God"* (Romans 10:17). If you continue to confess the Word of God, as an outgrowth of your desire to serve Him, you will eventually begin to see the manifestation of the fruits of your lips. Therefore, whenever you are tempted to speak a negative outcome concerning various matters in your life, confess the Word of God instead and hold fast to the confession of your faith.

> The more you receive the Word of God into your heart, the more your faith builds.

> *For the Scripture says, "Whoever believes on Him will not be put to shame."*
>
> (Romans 10:11)

Thousands of souls in hell are experiencing the shame of their actions, which have led to their eternal demise. As a believer, however, regardless of what threatens to expose your vulnerabilities and struggles, as long as you continue to believe and to seek the face of God, you will not be ashamed.

One time, after I had been praying for several days about many people whom I knew and loved who were in spiritual bondage, I had a vision. I saw heaven open and chariots charge out of it. A big, powerful angel was in each of the chariots. They all came down to the earth to help people who were in bondage and to deliver them. They went to the families that I had been praying for to set them free. My prayer is that if you are in spiritual bondage, you will reject Satan's demonic devices. You, too, have power over them in the name of Jesus. Demons tremble at Jesus' name and flee from His presence.

I often liken our relationship with God to many ships that make up the spiritual sea of our existence. He is the Captain of them all, and we are the passengers who embrace the ride with joy and gladness. One ship represents our fellowship with God, which He allows us to experience as we come to know our Lord and Savior Jesus Christ. Another ship represents our worship, where we are allowed to enter into the most sacred compartments of our Captain's quarters. Again, God does not cut Himself off from us when we commit wrongful acts. Rather, as we repent, He opens His doors and allows us access to His presence because of the sacrifice of His Son Jesus Christ on our behalf. In this way, we can reestablish our spiritual stand with Him.

It is imperative that I convey a clear message of the love of God and His desire to see you saved. When you repent from your heart before God Almighty and admit to Him your struggles and that you need deliverance in Jesus' name, He will hear you—wherever you are—and will deliver you and set you free.

The mistake many people make is thinking they have to overcome the wrong things in their lives before submitting to God and serving Him. The best thing to do is to give your heart to Jesus Christ now, repent of your sins, and allow Him to wash you clean. He went to the cross to save you from eternal damnation.

RECEIVE GOD'S OFFER OF MERCY

Many souls who are now in hell heard the gospel yet rejected its truth. They essentially chose hell by not believing in Jesus Christ and giving Him their whole heart and mind.

Do we really understand what eternal damnation is? In my visions, I saw that hell is a place of unrest and torment where the souls of people are doomed to live forever. The souls in hell long for a final death to eliminate their pain and torture, but it never comes. They scream for water and mercy, but nobody cares. Demons come up and stab at them while cursing obscenities, saying, "If you don't shut up, we will burn you more." I saw rats biting souls, and they screamed, "Help us! Get us out!" The cries of the dead are beyond belief, and the filthy odors are overwhelming.

Jesus came to earth to save us from this. That is why I am calling on you to repent of your sins and ask Christ to come into your heart, save your soul, and make you clean. We have no promise of life on earth tomorrow because no person knows the day he will die or the day when Christ will return.

> God has great mercy, and He is reaching out to you today.

The extent of God's love surpasses all human understanding. His mercy and grace still reach out to those who are committing terrible offenses, but it is up to each individual to receive His offer of repentance and to completely surrender his life over to God through Christ.

God wants you to know He has great mercy and that He is still reaching out to you today. If you are not yet a Christian, or if you are a Christian who is struggling with unbelief and the things of this world, there is deliverance for you in Jesus

Christ. Turn to Him, trust in Him, and surrender your life to Him completely.

> [Jesus said,] *All that the Father gives Me will come to Me, and the one who comes to Me I will by no means cast out.*
>
> (John 6:37)

> *If we confess our sins, He is faithful and just to forgive us our sins and to cleanse us from all unrighteousness.* (1 John 1:9)

> *Now may the God of peace Himself sanctify you completely; and may your whole spirit, soul, and body be preserved blameless at the coming of our Lord Jesus Christ.* ***He who calls you is faithful, who also will do it.*** (1 Thessalonians 5:23–24, emphasis added)

4

GUARDING YOUR CONFESSION OF FAITH

Scripture teaches that it is the Lord's will for us to remain blameless and to shine as lights in the world—revealing the love, grace, and power of God.

> *That you may become blameless and harmless, children of God without fault in the midst of a crooked and perverse generation, among whom you shine as lights in the world, holding fast the word of life.* (Philippians 2:15–16)

There are several truths and principles we need to follow in order to guard the confession of our faith and to shine as lights in the midst of this dark world.

BE AWARE OF YOUR ENEMY

When you receive Christ as Lord and Savior, you must become aware of the fact that there is an unseen evil realm whose purpose is to deceive you into returning to your old way of life. You may not want to deal with this reality, but ignoring it will not make it less real or cause it to go away. If you want more of God, and if you want to remain in Him, you have to continue your walk of faith and not give up when challenges arise. Everything I have is from being on my knees in prayer and pressing into God.

> **If you want more of God, you can't give up when challenges arrive.**

I remember a particularly difficult time. I was attempting to get my first book published on the topic of hell, and for various reasons, I was extremely discouraged. I had no money left to complete the project and I was very upset, so I said to myself, "I'm going to take this book down to the river and throw it in. There is no way I can get it published."

On the day I had decided to throw the manuscript into the river and forget about it, I was in bed dreaming when I felt a smack on my ankle. I looked around, but no one was there. All of a sudden, I was translated from the room and found myself standing in the galaxies, overlooking the earth.

Oh, my God! What have I done? I said to myself. I began to repent, saying, "Lord, this book is the work of the Holy Spirit! Please forgive me." Then I heard a voice say, "Who are you to be afraid of man? Child, I gave you the divine revelation of hell, and you shall go forth to share with others the reality of what I have shown. You shall also make a movie at the time appointed."

As I was listening to the voice of God and trembling, I looked over to my left and saw a huge ball of fire. Inside the flame I saw the outline of a face; it looked like molded iron. Fire came out of its eyes and shot up to the universe. Its jaws were like iron. Its mouth opened, fire came rushing out, and I screamed. Again, God said to me, "Who are you to be afraid of man, whom I created? They are like grasshoppers in My sight." He then said, "I'm going to put you back into the earth and you are going to do My will. You are not going to throw what I have given you into the river, and I will get the book published." And with that, I was back in my home, shouting and praising the Lord. I was terrified of what I had seen, yet I knew it was the Lord.

I thought to myself, *Who are we that we can manipulate God?* You have to be real and honest with Him. If you are sinning, tell Him you are a sinner. If you are doing things in the wrong way, then tell Him you are wrong and ask Him for instructions on how to change. God is concerned about the decisions that you make and is committed to assisting you in making the right choices when you seek Him for the proper guidance.

Become Established in Your Faith

Second, you must become established in your faith. God may send others to pray with you and to stand in the gap for you, but you must also pray for yourself. In addition, you must find a good church that believes in deliverance and the power of the Holy Spirit. I cannot stress enough the importance of staying in a church with a pastor who really cares about your soul and preaches the gospel without watering it down with what the carnal, or fleshly, mind wants to hear.

> The Bible is your main weapon for destroying the devil's kingdom.

You also have to read the Bible for yourself. The Bible is your main weapon for destroying the devil's kingdom. It is a tool you can use to mature in your faith and become wise concerning both the devices of Satan and the blessings of God.

When you are confronted by the demonic warfare of Satan's kingdom, you will be better equipped to maintain your deliverance if you are receiving a continuous impartation of the truth concerning the power of God.

A person who has the righteousness of Christ has the right to reign with God forever. The devil knows this, which is why he attempts to get you to speak everything except the Word of God over your life. The devil knows that in the confession of your faith lies life-giving sustenance and power. To maintain your confession, therefore, counteract the devil's ploy by speaking the Word of God. This is what Jesus did when He was tempted by the devil after fasting and praying for forty days. When the devil came to tempt him, He answered him only with Scripture.

The biggest mistakes people make when confronted with Satan's temptations are (1) giving up and indulging in the temptation the devil is offering, and (2) wasting time going back and forth arguing with the devil when they should be taking authority over him. There is no use trying to convince the devil of your spiritual strength. He already knows the power of Christ that lies within you. This is why he attempts to use deceitful tactics of distraction to prevent you from using that power over him. Instead, *"submit to God. Resist the devil and he will flee from you"* (James 4:7). Counteract his deception with the truth of God's Word.

KEEP SPIRITUALLY AWARE AND STRONG

Scripture also admonishes us to work out our own salvation with *"fear and trembling"*:

Therefore, my beloved, as you have always obeyed, not as in my presence only, but now much more in my absence, work out your own salvation with fear and trembling; for it is God who works in you both to will and to do for His good pleasure.
(Philippians 2:12–13)

Why does verse 12 include the phrase *"with fear and trembling"*? I believe God wants us to realize there is a price to pay for living a lawless and careless lifestyle and dying without repentance. With all the love, joy, and peace that God offers us, there is no justifiable reason to reject Him.

People who have strayed from God often say things like, "I'm done with the church! I'm going to do what I want and whenever I want to do it." We should never love an institution so much thatwe turn away from God when it hurts us. Bitterness is a demonic attack that is strategically designed by the enemy to trick you into resenting

God. Nothing or no one should be so important to you that it becomes powerful enough to threaten the stability of your spiritual stand with God. Hatred and unforgiveness are deceitful forces that come from the gates of hell to annihilate your confession of faith and to keep you as far away as possible from the will of God.

Think about it. What better breeding ground for contention among Christians is there than the church? The local church is the place where the believers of God spend much of their time. We improve our lives and raise our children in the church. We gather there for support in the midst of crises. So much of our lives is invested there. Is it any great surprise, then, that the enemy is using this place, which is meant to bring us strength, to expose our weaknesses and use them against us?

> **The church should bring us strength, but the enemy uses it to expose our weaknesses.**

The devil wants the world to look at the church and see divisiveness in order to give people more ammunition to stay as far away from God as possible. This is a trick of the enemy that, unfortunately, many churchgoers and even church leaders often fail to see. Just as there is a very real heaven that God would like us to see, there is also a very real place called hell that the devil would like us to be condemned to forever. As the devil continues to use everyday aspects of our lives to distract us from the will of God, demons in hell are laughing at the souls who are being exported into the gates of hell. These invisible portals are hungry for souls and will stop at nothing to carry out their plans of deceit.

Remain Focused on the Essentials

In keeping spiritually aware and strong, we also must focus on these three aspects of our walk with Christ, because God's judgment of us will be based on them:

1. The *truth* of God's Word.
2. The *belief* and *confession* of our hearts.
3. The *actions* that follow from our confession.

Keep to the Truth of God's Word

First, keep to the truth of God's Word because regardless of how much the world changes, the Word of God remains the same:

For I am the LORD, I do not change.
(Malachi 3:6)

The grass withers, the flower fades, but the word of our God stands forever.
(Isaiah 40:8)

*The entirety of Your word is truth, and
every one of Your righteous judgments endures forever.*   (Psalm 119:160)

But the word of the LORD endures forever.
                                        (1 Peter 1:25)

What truth should you believe about salvation? It is revealed in Romans 10:9: *"If you confess with your mouth the Lord Jesus **and believe**
in your heart that God has raised Him from the
dead, you will be saved"* (emphasis added). We
must know that salvation comes only through
Christ. Today, more than ever, we must maintain
a firm stand against demonic strongholds and
know, without a doubt, in whom we believe and in
what we believe.

*See to it that no one takes you captive
through hollow and deceptive philosophy,
which depends on human tradition and
the basic principles of this world rather
than on Christ.*   (Colossians 2:8 NIV)

Likewise, whenever you are in doubt about
how to respond to something in your life, you can
always refer to the Word of God to measure the
appropriateness of your actions. The ordinances
in God's Word serve as a road map, not only to
lead us to salvation, but also to guide us in our

everyday lives so that we live according to His will. They teach us how to be good wives or husbands, how to treat our children and parents, and how to avoid being deceived by the devices of Satan.

In our own strength, many of the things that we go through in life seem absolutely unconquerable.

> The trials of life may seem unconquerable, but with God, nothing is impossible.

Yet nothing is impossible to those who believe in God and His love and power. (See Mark 9:23.) When we sincerely turn to Him in prayer, God hears us and sends help. Therefore, we should do our best to obey God in everything He tells us to do.

Have a Heart of True Belief

Second, make sure you have a heart of true belief. Regardless of how much we claim to be in right standing with God, ultimately, it is the condition of our hearts that will determine the veracity of our confessions.

As we have seen, both belief and confession are vital for salvation:

> *If you confess with your mouth the Lord Jesus and believe in your heart that God*

*has raised Him from the dead, you will
be saved. For with the heart one believes
unto righteousness, and with the mouth
confession is made unto salvation.*

(Romans 10:9–10)

We can confess faith in Christ with our mouths
all we want. Yet if the Word of God has not also
dwelled in our hearts, so that our confession is
genuine, we will be made aware of the error of our
ways during God's judgment.

*For the Lord does not see as man sees; for
man looks at the outward appearance, but
the LORD looks at the heart.*

(1 Samuel 16:7)

All too often, we judge a person's spiritual
stand based upon what we see outwardly. Nevertheless, God looks past the physical façade
and peers directly into the heart. The prophet
Samuel almost made the mistake of looking at
outward appearance in choosing a king for Israel from the household of Jesse based upon the
physical stature of Jesse's sons. Yet the Lord was
quick to correct him. He caused Samuel to look
past the physicality of each of the older sons and
instead to see through the eyes of God to recognize the youngest son, David, as the upcoming
king of Israel.

When God judges, He looks at the heart.

Let Your Actions Match Your Confession

Third, make sure your actions match your confession. We are justified by faith, but we are also to do good works as an outgrowth and evidence of our faith. Remember that your works don't save you. However, you cannot say you truly have a relationship with Jesus if you continue to disobey Him and aren't doing the works He calls you to do.

> *For we are His workmanship, created in Christ Jesus for good works, which God prepared beforehand that we should walk in them.* (Ephesians 2:10)

> *Those who have believed in God should be careful to maintain good works.*
> (Titus 3:8)

> *As the body without the spirit is dead, so faith without works is dead also.*
> (James 2:26)

It's not enough just to confess Jesus as Lord; we must also make a conscious effort to adhere to His commands and do good works. We are to seek the things that are above, not the things of the earth. (See Colossians 3:1–2.) Our life is to be *"hidden with Christ in God"* (v. 3). We are to *"put on the new man who is renewed in knowledge according to the image of* [Christ]*"* (v. 10).

God gives us faith (see Romans 12:3) in order to carry out His good will. Let us put God before all else; let us treat others with godly love and show mercy, grace, and forgiveness, just as our Lord and Savior administers these gifts to us.

LIVING BY FAITH

Finally, it is imperative to remember that Christ is the one and only, true and living Judge. We are never to assess someone's salvation (including our own) based only on his or her struggles. Each of us has a unique relationship with Christ through which He determines His final judgment. Paul wrote in Romans 14:4, *"Who are you to judge another's servant? To his own master he stands or falls. Indeed, he will be made to stand, for God is able to make him stand."*

> Let us treat others with mercy, grace, and forgiveness, just as God gives these gifts to us.

This is not to say that the Lord casually tolerates a sinful lifestyle. If you are in the midst of wrongdoing, God's grace is available to you so that you can turn away from it. However, if you persist in it, you are breaking the commandment of God. Do not be deceived into thinking you are born again and are going to heaven if you continue to sin without repentance.

> We know [absolutely] that anyone born of God does not [deliberately and knowingly] practice committing sin, but the One Who was begotten of God carefully watches over and protects him [Christ's divine presence within him preserves him against the evil], and the wicked one does not lay hold (get a grip) on him or touch [him].
>
> (1 John 5:18 AMP)

> If we say that we have fellowship with Him, and walk in darkness, we lie and do not practice the truth. But if we walk in the light as He is in the light, we have fellowship with one another, and the blood of Jesus Christ His Son cleanses us from all sin. If we say that we have no sin, we deceive ourselves, and the truth is not in us.
> (1 John 1:6–8)

God's grace is available to us. *"If we confess our sins, He is faithful and just to forgive us our sins and to cleanse us from all unrighteousness"* (1 John 1:9). Furthermore, God has given each of us a measure of faith; we are to strengthen our faith according to His Word and activate that faith, in order to remain in righteousness.

> *For I say, through the grace given to me, to everyone who is among you, not to think of himself more highly than he ought to think, but to think soberly, as God has dealt to each one a measure of faith.*
>
> (Romans 12:3)

> *So then faith comes by hearing, and hearing by the word of God.*   (Romans 10:17)

> *The just [*"righteous" NIV*] shall live by faith.*   (Romans 1:17)

5

RECOGNIZING AND COUNTERACTING DEMONIC TACTICS

God does not want us to be in bondage to the enemy and his schemes. We have a God who loves us so much He provided a way of freedom in the name of Jesus Christ and by His blood. He truly wants to deliver you from the hand of Satan. Therefore, He wants you to understand the reality of the demonic deception and the tactics associated with the gates of hell—and how to counteract them.

The Lord is an awesome God, and He can carry you through whatever dilemma presents itself in your life. When you know who you are in Christ Jesus, nothing can stop you—not even the deceptive devices of Satan's kingdom that come to kill, steal, and destroy. (See John 10:10.) Again, this is why it is vitally important for you to be under the leadership of a church that presents biblical teaching, since much of the world today rejects the teachings of Jesus Christ. There are truths concerning the kingdom of darkness and spiritual warfare that you must learn in order to recognize and thwart the attacks of Satan.

SATANIC INFLUENCES

From the average citizen to the most prominent figure in society, no one—without the power of God—is impervious to the influences of Satan's manipulative forces. Hell has much deception, seduction, and evil. Even the demons do not trust each other. They cannot believe each other because they are all liars.

The devil is not going to do anything that will be beneficial to your existence, but will wage spiritual warfare against you in order to destroy you. The difficulties you are currently experiencing in your life may not be human battles at all. Rather, they may be spiritual strongholds caused by demonic powers in order to beguile or discourage you into relinquishing your royal inheritance as a king and priest in God's kingdom. Jesus provided this inheritance for us, and we are to guard it. In the book of Revelation, we read,

[Jesus] *has made us kings and priests to His God and Father.* (Revelation 1:6)

[Jesus has] *made us kings and priests to our God; and we shall reign on the earth.*
(Revelation 5:10)

Do not allow the enemy to steal what God has given you.

SPIRITUAL WICKEDNESS IN HIGH PLACES

The unseen truth we all must understand is that spiritual wickedness rules over various territories. If the rulers of darkness are not cast down, they will govern whatever yields to their demonic influences within those territories.

In one vision, I saw demonic powers hovering over a certain state. They were huge creatures—perhaps fifty feet tall—and they were resting upon seven large cement thrones. They were all in a circle, mumbling to each other. They tried to imitate the authoritative voice of God, which is like the sound of many waters. (See Revelation 1:15; 14:2.) Because God had already allowed me to hear His voice when He took me into heaven, I recognized that although this contrary voice was very similar to the one I had heard, it was not the same.

The true and living God said to me, "It sounds similar to My voice, child, doesn't it?" He explained, "This is the prince of the power of the air, the rulers of demon darkness, the spiritual wickedness in high places that sit in the heavens above the earth. They cause chaos in the lives of people and brainwash those who acquiesce to their ungodly influences. I want you to see this, understand it, and tell the world about it. Explain to them that in the name of Jesus they have the authority and the power to pull this evil kingdom down."

I soon began to understand the reality and necessity of the spiritual armor Paul wrote about in Ephesians 6. Paul exhorted us to always be spiritually dressed for battle in order to counter-act demonic attacks and strongholds.

Put on the whole armor of God, that you may be able to stand against the wiles of the devil. For we do not wrestle against flesh and blood, but against principali-ties, against powers, against the rulers of the darkness of this age, against spiri-tual hosts of wickedness in the heavenly places. (Ephesians 6:11–12)

As I prepared to pray, the Lord reminded me, "Whatever you bind on earth is bound in heaven, and whatever you loose on earth is loosed in heaven. [See Matthew 16:19; 18:18.] Take dominion over these things and bind them. Command them to fall off their thrones, in the name of Jesus, and by the blood of Jesus Christ."

Jesus said that if we believe in Him, we can accomplish even greater works on earth than He did, through the power of the Holy Spirit: *"Most assuredly, I say to you, he who believes in Me, the works that I do he will do also; and greater works than these he will do, because I go to My Father"* (John 14:12). As God reveals the kingdom of darkness to us, we can truly exercise our power to prevail over every demonic attack. I think it is wonderful that God has

> God has endowed us with His power, which exalts the Lord Jesus Christ.

endowed us with His power—not that we are exalted, but that we exalt the Lord Jesus Christ.

As I watched these evil forms manifest upon their cement thrones, I knew that many people were going to be deceived on the earth. So I began to pray to God and praise Him for deliverance. Then I saw a group of angels descending from heaven. I saw them circle these demons, put chains around them, and yank them from their thrones. One by one, they began to fall off their thrones as the angels of God dragged them away. The angels were shouting and praising the Lord in the name of Jesus Christ.

Through the blood of Jesus and in His name, we can defeat every demon. In the sport of bowling, the object is to knock down the bowling pins that are lined up at the end of the lane. As you throw the ball toward the pins, the ball may sometimes roll into the gutter. But your goal is to hit the front pin so that it will fall and knock over all the other pins as well. This is the way I look at spiritual warfare against demons. If we deal with evil spirits directly, by striking them with the name of Jesus Christ, they will respond by falling over in defeat. They will flee because they cannot stand against the name of Jesus and the blood He shed on our behalf.

Let us now look at some key elements to recognizing spiritual attacks.

OPERATIONS OF DEMONS

Deception through False Teaching

As I wrote in chapter one, the devil uses the strategy of deception to entrap people and destroy them, and one of the ways he deceives is through false teaching. It is no coincidence that there are so many books and other materials available today on how to "realize your full potential." We are being taught to hear from our "inner voice" while ignoring the voice of God. This is not to say that we shouldn't continually seek to learn more about ourselves and the world around us, and to improve our lives. Yet many teachings in the popular culture negate the reality of God and His Word while promoting the supposed superiority of humanity and human beings' own intellectual and "spiritual" abilities. We must be cautious that we do not buy into these ideas, which are based upon the flawed opinions of fallen humanity rather than on the truth of God's Word.

Anytime we fail to recognize God's voice or mistake the devil's voice for God's voice, demons rejoice at our ignorance. When we lend our ears to the devil's voice, we can risk our inheritance, just as Adam and Eve lost their inheritance to the devil when they listened to his lies in the garden of Eden.

> **We must learn to recognize God's voice so we won't accept the devil's counterfeit.**

Satan wants to trick you into giving away your spiritual standing by using tactics of manipulation and intimidation. He uses the fact that people are searching for God as an opportunity to present them with a form of godliness that actually has no power. (See 2 Timothy 3:5.) In the last days, many teachings will be made available to us disguised as godly and pure counsel. We will be presented with all types of doctrines that seek to open our minds to receive erroneous gospels. This is why the truth and wisdom of God's Word is such a vital source to those who already believe, as well as for those who are searching for God.

We must be able to discern erroneous teaching from the true gospel of Jesus Christ. Our inheritance is not hell's gates but eternal life.

The Spirit Himself bears witness with our spirit that we are children of God, and if children, then heirs; heirs of God and joint heirs with Christ, if indeed we suffer with Him, that we may also be glorified together. (Romans 8:16–17)

The following are some guidelines that will help us to distinguish the difference between biblical truth and error.

1. *Does the teaching say that salvation is found only in Jesus Christ?* Today we are inundated with teachings about all types of "gods" and "prophets" through whom we are supposed to find truth and salvation. Some of these teachings even promote the idea that we ourselves are "gods" or "goddesses." If the teaching encourages the deification or worship of anyone other than God the Father, His Son Jesus Christ, and the Holy Spirit, then it is

not the true gospel. Moreover, if another man or woman claims to be the Christ, he or she is presenting an erroneous gospel. (See, for example, Acts 4:10–12; Jeremiah 10:11–12; Matthew 24:4–5.)

2. *Does the teaching affirm that Jesus was born of a virgin, led a sinless life, died for our sins, and was physically resurrected?* Any teaching that contradicts even one of these biblical doctrines is an erroneous gospel. (See, for example, Isaiah 7:14; Hebrews 4:15; 1 Corinthians 15:3–4.)

3. *Does the teaching deny the reality of the physical body of man or the eternal spirit of man?* Humanity consists of body, soul, and spirit, and the human spirit is eternal. *"It is appointed for men to die once, but after this the judgment"* (Hebrews 9:27). After we die, we are not reincarnated as another human being or as an animal. Our eternal destination is determined forever by the decisions we make while upon the earth. (See, for example, 1 Thessalonians 5:23; 2 Corinthians 5:1; Matthew 25:31–46; Mark 16:16.)

4. *Does the teaching claim to know the date the world will end?* If the teaching makes such a claim, it is not the authentic gospel of Christ, because Jesus said no one knows the day or

the hour at which He will return. (See, for example, Matthew 24:36; 25:13.)

Preying on People's Vulnerability

Another operation of demons is to prey on the vulnerability of both Christians and non-Christians. When I was taken into hell, I saw groups of demons speaking. They were huddled together in groups consisting of twelve to twenty demons, and the largest demon of each group was giving the others orders to carry out on the earth. I saw a group of ten smaller demons whose job was to go upon the earth to a certain state in America and wreak havoc in the lives of the family members of powerful men and women of God.

There was one minister, in particular, whom I saw the demons discussing. They had been assigned the job of attacking this minister's cousin in order to distract the minister from doing the will of God. The order went out to cause accidents in the cousin's life. "We want you to cause accidents and problems because this minister is not watching and praying, nor is he reading his Bible. He is not covered with the Word of God, so I want you to expose an issue that he has in his life." The demons were giggling and laughing, and they couldn't wait to do this. They offered rewards to other demons for accomplishing even more turmoil.

As I was listening to this, I heard the largest demon say to a group of demons that were about ten feet tall, "Your job is to go and cause total chaos and hardships in their finances. You are the 'strong man,' and you are going to cause a lot of divisions in the marriages of this family, and this, too, will distract the minister." (See, for example, Matthew 12:29.) They warned each other that the minister would eventually become concerned about his cousin and begin to pray. "He has the power in the name of...the name we don't like to say...he has power in that name to cast you out, but if you go and do these things quickly before he has time to discern or pray, we can invoke damaging crises to prevail over this family."

> God knows everything the devil is planning, and He is ready to send us help.

This minister did not know that all this chattering and scheming was going on in order to tear down his family. He did not know he should pray and begin seeking the Lord diligently. Nevertheless, the angels of God heard this plan, and protective angels were sent. While these demonic schemes were being planned, God already had a plan in place to send a group of angels to protect both this individual and his family. God is brilliant.

He knows everything the devil is doing, and He knows how to send help from His sanctuary. (See Psalm 20:1–2.) If you read the book of Psalms, you will notice that He has done this many times.

Much as they tried to do in the minister's life, the operation of demons is to wreak havoc and cause annoyances in your life that are so overwhelming you will focus your attention solely on what is going on around you. They try to keep you from remaining diligent in prayer and maintaining a state of faithfulness and obedience to God. For example, they may cause your automobile to break down and your electric bill to be increased beyond comprehension right when you are trying to come up with enough money to pay the mortgage on your home. These evil presences try to attack anything that we deal with in the natural world in order to destroy our spirits.

Demons will attack vulnerable children as well as vulnerable adults. For instance, if a child is being raped or otherwise abused, she usually has so much fear and torment in her heart and mind that demonic spirits come to keep her in a state of bewilderment and low self-esteem throughout her entire life. She can often break free only by deliverance through the grace of God and in the name of Jesus. That is what deliverance is all about—setting the captives free.

Another vulnerable area is many people's lack of understanding of the true nature of spiritual warfare. They think it is always rare or dramatic, and so they shy away from it. Or they argue about what spiritual warfare really involves. Instead, we must realize that we all confront spiritual warfare practically every day. The devil's attacks against both believers and nonbelievers are relentless because he desires to keep us from our heavenly Father.

There is unseen warfare going on in the heavenly realm that we actively take part in, often without even realizing it. For instance, have you ever said to yourself, "Tomorrow, I am going on a fast"? Even

> **We must realize we all confront spiritual warfare practically every day.**

if you normally skip breakfast, when you wake up the morning of your fast, you are so hungry that you find yourself holding a doughnut in your hand before you even remember that this is the day you had promised to sacrifice to God. This type of circumstance is usually not coincidental. The devil will use whatever vulnerability he can find to tempt you to breach your faithfulness to God. During a fast, he may tempt you with food; in times of financial lack, he may bombard your mind with the fear of unpaid bills; in illness, he may intensify the pain; and in grief, he may cause oppression.

Tempting People to Make Bad Decisions

Another trick of the enemy is to use your appetite for earthly things to get you to compromise or neglect your spiritual stand with God through foolish decisions. Making a bad decision based on earthly desires, therefore, not only can potentially have an adverse effect on your family, job, or economic status, but it can also sometimes devastate your relationship with the Lord.

When you are tempted to make a decision based on unbiblical motivations, recognize that your spiritual health is at stake. Seek God's guidance in prayer and look to His Word when making decisions. Do not think through only the material consequences of your decision, but also the spiritual consequences.

Sometimes, we make negative, life-altering decisions simply because we do not heed the voice of God. When God speaks, it is for a specific purpose, so always take time listen to what He has to say. Never become so busy in life that you no longer have time to hear God's voice.

Hell's gates are not to be the reigning force behind the believer's decision-making process.

When you take the time to get to know God, you are also able to experience the dominion that He has given you over the earth through the Holy Spirit and the name of Jesus, and the gates of hell are incapable of prevailing against you.

Encouraging People to React Badly to Life's Crises

The enemy would also like us to nurture uncontrolled emotions so that we will react to life's crises according to our feelings rather than according to God's Word. For example, in the midst of a crisis, the worst thing you can do is to respond or to make a life-altering decision while enraged. Rage is the devil's playground, and he will use it to his full advantage. Many who become intoxicated with anger have great remorse after sobering from their indulgence in this potentially poisonous emotion. They say things like, "I don't know what came over me."

Always take time to walk away from a situation that is out of control instead of resorting to handling it without the assistance of God. Remember what the Scripture says: *"Be angry, and do not sin": do not let the sun go down on your wrath, nor give place to the devil"* (Ephesians 4:26–27). We may find ourselves angry in certain situations, but we are not to sin by becoming enraged, seeking vengeance, or harboring unforgiveness. We are not to give the devil any opening to work in our lives.

Trapping People through Spiritual Strongholds

Another job of demonic forces is to affect our behavior through "strongholds." Generally defined, a stronghold is a supporting beam or a fortress that people build to keep their enemies out. Our enemy is the devil. Yet the devil's enemy is anything that pertains to godliness and truth, and he tries to create strongholds in your life that will block godliness and truth from reigning there.

Satanic strongholds may be manifested in the form of "generational curses." These are strongholds that often take hold under a certain name or a particular problem or ailment, such as abuse or addiction. These strongholds are passed along in families and may date back to your great-grandparents or even earlier.

Again, demonic forces may try to bind you in a certain area in order to prevent the Spirit of God and His blessings from fully manifesting in your life. To bind means to firmly tie up. If strongholds are never confronted by a spiritually mature person who knows how to take authority over them, they may become resident forces of evil that stubbornly refuse to give up their domain. For example, when a person binds himself or herself to the wrong person in marriage and becomes one with that person, he or she sometimes begins to inherit many of the negative traits of the spouse.

Territorial demons may have the "right" to bind you in certain areas due to the generational curses that have been allowed to fester in the family throughout the years—unless you overcome them through the name and blood of Christ, who took the punishment for them on the cross to set you free. You therefore have to take authority over these strongholds through Christ in order to experience liberty. Unless you cast them down, they will likely continue to fester in your life and in succeeding generations.

> **We can counteract Satan by the blood of Christ and the Word of God.**

COUNTERACTING DEMONIC ATTACKS AND STRONGHOLDS

Satan refuses to give up his rule over this world without a strategic fight. We can counteract him and his cohorts by the name and blood of Christ, by the power of the Word of God, and by living according to God's ways. Here are some ways to protect yourself from strongholds, as well as to wage spiritual warfare.

Live under God's Protection

In order to be protected from Satan's strongholds and other devices, you must live in a place of safety built by the Master Architect—the Lord Jesus Christ. The shelter He provides is (1) capable of sustaining you, and (2) strong enough to keep the enemy from penetrating your confession of faith. This place of safety has a foundation built on the true gospel of salvation through Jesus Christ, the living Word of God.

According to the grace of God which was given to me, as a wise master builder I have laid the foundation, and another builds on it. But let each one take heed how he builds on it. For no other foundation can anyone lay than that which is laid, which is Jesus Christ.

(1 Corinthians 3:10–11)

Since you have purified your souls in obeying the truth through the Spirit in sincere love of the brethren, love one another fervently with a pure heart, having been born again, not of corruptible seed but incorruptible, through the word of God which lives and abides forever. (1 Peter 1:22–23)

Anytime your spiritual foundation becomes shaky, it is because you are mixing it with something that does not belong. Check out what-ever is contaminating your foundation. Are you listening to the wrong voices, taking bad advice, or doubting the strength of God's Word?

Your Master Architect understands the ne-cessity of having a structure that can protect you from turbulent winds and rains—the tests and trials of life. Within your strong fortress are sup-porting beams built by the Master Architect to help sustain it. The lessons of life teach us to stay put under the protection of the fortress during tu-multuous seasons!

These beams of protection can be removed only by the delicate hands of God. He may do so temporarily, as He did with the patriarch Job, to fulfill His purposes, after which He will restore them. However, if you remove these beams of pro-tection on your own, through spiritual neglect or pride, this can cause the entire structure to col-lapse—with you inside.

Again, these beams have been strategically placed in the dwelling to sustain the structure of your existence and to keep you close to God. He wants to talk to you and dwell with you in the innermost places of your personal existence. He uses these times to impart divine wisdom to you before releasing you into the world to face de-monic elements that desire to sift you like wheat.

(See Luke 22:31–32.) This is why Psalm 91:1–2 is such a powerful revelation:

He who dwells in the secret place of the Most High shall abide under the shadow of the Almighty. I will say of the Lord, "He is my refuge and my fortress; My God, in Him I will trust."

In this passage, the psalmist revealed the omnipotence of God. It does not matter where we are or what type of demonic strongholds come against us, God is always right there with us to give us the victory. There is no place too dark for the light of God to shine and reveal His marvelous power of deliverance. (See Psalm 139:7–12.) We do not have to be afraid of the attacks of the enemy, for they are no match for the power of God residing within us through His Spirit.

Beloved, do not believe every spirit, but test the spirits, whether they are of God; because many false prophets have gone out into the world. By this you know the Spirit of God: Every spirit that confesses that Jesus Christ has come in the flesh is of God, and every spirit that does not confess that Jesus Christ has come in the flesh is not of God. And this is the spirit of the Antichrist, which you have heard was

*coming, and is now already in the world.
You are of God, little children, and have
overcome them, because He who is in you
is greater than he who is in the world.*
(1 John 4:1–4, emphasis added)

Remember the confident and comforting
words of King David:

*Yea, though I walk through the valley of
the shadow of death, I will fear no evil; for
You are with me; Your rod and Your staff,
they comfort me.* (Psalm 23:4)

David did not fear death because he knew it
was no match for God. When his opponent Goliath showed up, even though Goliath's large, shadowy figure eclipsed the sun, not even this would
prevent David from taking off his enemy's head.
He understood that anything looks larger in the
shadows. He was so bold that he even warned Goliath of his impending death. Because David had
spent time in the secret places with God Almighty,
he was not intimidated by this public display of
demonic intimidation. (See 1 Samuel 17.)

Know That Christ Has Already Won the Victory

*"For we do not wrestle against flesh and
blood, but against...the rulers of the darkness of
this age, against spiritual hosts of wickedness*

in the heavenly places" (Ephesians 6:12). Today, most "professional" wrestling matches are predetermined. The one who is favored drives the outcome of the match. In a similar way, the spiritual wrestling matches that we deal with have already been predetermined by God. Whether you know it or not, the battle that you are presently in is "fixed"; in God's eyes, you have already won the fight because of Christ's complete victory over the devil—as long as you remain spiritually strong and rely on Him. We must recognize that we are favored to win because we belong to the one who is the Victor.

> *For this purpose the Son of God was manifested, that He might destroy the works of the devil.* (1 John 3:8)

> *When* [Jesus] *ascended on high, He led captivity captive.* (Ephesians 4:8)

To be effective in spiritual warfare, therefore, you must know who you are in Christ. If you have been born again, you are His child, you belong to Him, and Christ has already won the victory for you. When you belong to God, even though it seems as if you are getting knocked around and are losing, you can know that you are already wearing the winner's belt because Christ has destroyed the works of the devil.

Maintain Fellowship with the Heavenly Father

We gain knowledge about defeating the devil by fellowshipping with God in the Spirit. Fellowshipping with God means acknowledging Him in all our ways. God will sometimes allow us to encounter difficulties that He knows can be overcome only by His Spirit so that we will learn to rely on Him.

I have also found that God sometimes allows us to be caught up in smaller storms and to experience bumps and bruises in order to protect us from larger storms that have the potential of actually "killing" us. Moreover, the storms in our lives may have been allowed by God for a season in order to build us up for what lies ahead. The "hell" that you are going through right now may be for the purpose of strengthening you with wisdom to endure future crises.

> If you are born again, you are God's child, and Christ has already won the victory for you.

In Acts 27, the apostle Paul was on a boat heading for Rome, where he was to testify before Caesar. The Holy Spirit told him a storm was coming that would destroy the boat, but that everyone on board would be rescued. Likewise, in your life, before the "storm," God prepares you, and if you can hold on to His Word, you can make it through. God has called you and prepared you so that regardless of how turbulently the winds of life may blow, you can live and mature rather than be destroyed.

By worshipping our faithful Father in the midst of life's storms, we can float through adversities. He is the Lord of the storm as well as the Lord of the harvest. (See Mark 4:35–41.) He is the strength of our lives. (See Psalm 27:1.)

Seek God's Kingdom First

To avoid being ensnared by the cares of the world and becoming spiritually weak, do not worry about the material goods you do or do not have. Take your eyes off what you see in the physical and trust in God to provide for you as you seek His kingdom first in your life. Jesus said,

> Do not worry, saying, "What shall we eat?" or "What shall we drink?" or "What shall we wear?" For after all these things the Gentiles seek. For your heavenly Father knows that you need all these things. But seek first the kingdom of God and His righteousness, and all these things shall be added to you. (Matthew 6:31–33)

As you trust in your heavenly Father, His presence will come upon your life and rest on you. If you have been relying on yourself or others more than on Him, He may first rebuke you and then remind you, "I have already spoken the rest of your life into existence. I have given you your marching orders. If you want to know what you should do, ask Me."

Develop a lifestyle of seeking first the kingdom, and all your needs will be supplied. Activate the words of Romans 4:17 and believe God, who *"calls those things which do not exist as though they did."* Speak what you want according to His Word, write it down, and declare it to be so.

Maintain Your Faith in God

When the devil sets his mind to destroy you, he may constantly remind you of failures or setbacks from your past in order to discourage you and get you to give up on your future. Always remember that your spiritual health depends upon your holding on to your faith in God, even if that faith seems small to you. As you do this, realize that it is difficult to stay close to God if you are continually around people who are not committed to God themselves.

Trust in God's Commitment to You

Finally, my brethren, be strong in the Lord and in the power of His might.
                                    (Ephesians 6:10)

When you are under demonic assault, people may call you a failure or say you do not have enough faith because they do not realize why you are under such an attack. Yet you belong to God, and He remains committed to setting you free and purifying your mind. The apostle Paul wrote,

Now may the God of peace Himself sanctify you completely; and may your whole spirit, soul, and body be preserved blameless at the coming of our Lord Jesus Christ. He who calls you is faithful, who also will do it. (1 Thessalonians 5:23–24)

Everything you will be able to achieve and to conquer spiritually will be due to the strength of God that dwells within you. No matter what the crisis is, you can know that *"all things work together for good to those who love God, to those who are the called according to His purpose"* (Romans 8:28).

God is truly revealed in the midst of crises. When you come through to the other side of a dilemma, you may contemplate all that you have gone through and ask, "How did I ever get through that?" The strength of God was made perfect during your weakest moments. (See 2 Corinthians 12:9.)

Allow the Word of God to Sustain You

You must be prepared with the truth and power of God's Word in order to stand boldly in His righteousness and to war against the demonic strongholds of Satan's kingdom. If you speak His Word over your life, He is committed to seeing you through to the other side of the storms in your life. Utilize the power of confessing God's Word, and watch as His miraculous power begins to be revealed in your life. Confess...

- "I am the righteousness of God." (See 2 Corinthians 5:21.)
- "Jesus' blood covers my household." (See Exodus 12:13; Acts 16:31.)
- "No weapon formed against me will prosper." (See Isaiah 54:17.)
- "I can do all things through Christ." (See Philippians 4:13.)

Immediately after you make these confessions, demons may try to keep the blessings of God and the positive words of faith that you have spoken from manifesting in your life. Even so, you must continue to *"stand against the wiles of the devil"* (Ephesians 6:11) and remind yourself that God has spoken words over your life that cannot fail.

Not only can you have heaven when you die, but you can also experience heaven on earth by allowing His will to be done in your life here, as it is already done in heaven. (See Matthew 6:10; Luke 11:2.) Though you eat the bread of adversity and drink the water of affliction, His divine Word will sustain you. God says He is going to bring you out on top. (See Isaiah 30:20–21.) Do not ever believe that God has turned you over to the devil.

> **Confessing God's Word reveals His miraculous power in your life.**

Wage Spiritual Warfare through God's Power

We must always remember that there is nothing we can do by our own human means to counteract the satanic attacks in our lives. Only God can do this. God sometimes pulls down strongholds before we even recognize that they need to be pulled down. Other times, He wants us to recognize and pull them down in His power.

For the weapons of our warfare are not carnal but mighty in God for pulling down strongholds, casting down arguments and every high thing that exalts itself against the knowledge of God, bringing every thought into captivity to the obedience of Christ. (2 Corinthians 10:4–5)

The key to spiritual warfare in this verse is the phrase *"mighty in God."* For example, I never advise casting out demons without being sure of who you are in Christ. If demons do not recognize your authority in the heavenly realm, and you attempt to cast them out of someone, they will try to destroy both you and the person who is possessed. (See, for example, Acts 19:13–17.) You should never put another person's life in danger by playing the hero in a situation over which you have no control.

Jesus never fought with demons. He simply spoke a word and cast them out. (See, for example, Matthew 8:16.) He could do this because He walked in the authority of the Father. You cannot be intimidated by the hideousness of the gates of hell. Mathew reminds us that all power in heaven and in the earth was given to Jesus. (See Matthew 28:18 KJV.) If the Spirit of God resides in you, then you hold the power through Christ Jesus to come against the principalities, the powers, and the rulers of the darkness of this age, and to cast out demons in His name.

In the book of Jude, we read that when Moses died, God told the archangel Michael to bury the patriarch. Yet the devil went searching for Moses' body, apparently so that he could try to rule the children of Israel. Michael did not waste time with a *"reviling ["railing"* KJV] *accusation"* against the devil, but simply announced to him, *"The Lord rebuke you!"* (Jude 9).

It is never a good idea to argue with the devil. If you do, you will likely allow him to win the fight. You cannot defeat him with the weapons of human speech and reasoning. We should follow Michael's example when waging spiritual warfare, rebuking Satan in the name of Jesus in order to cast down every stronghold that the enemy uses as an attempt to keep us bound.

> **As you mature in faith, the Lord will teach you to dress in the full armor of God.**

As you mature in your faith, you must also learn to put on the full armor of God to counteract the enemy's schemes. In Ephesians 6:11, we read, *"Put on the whole armor of God, that you may be able to stand against the wiles of the devil."* Then the Lord teaches us how to dress for battle:

> *Therefore take up the whole armor of God, that you may be able to withstand in the evil day, and having done all, to stand. Stand therefore, having girded your waist with **truth**, having put on the breastplate of **righteousness**, and having shod your feet with the **preparation of the gospel of***

*peace; above all, taking the shield of **faith**
with which you will be able to quench all
the fiery darts of the wicked one. And take
the helmet of **salvation**, and the sword of
the Spirit, which is the word of God.*
(Ephesians 6:13–17, emphasis added)

The armor of God includes...

• Truth
• Righteousness
• Preparation
• Faith
• Salvation

Your spiritual armor will protect you, and
your training in spiritual warfare will guide you
as you battle the enemy's tactics.

Rely on God's Grace

When we are weak, the grace of God steps in
to give us the strength that we need to make it.

*My grace is sufficient for you, for My
strength is made perfect in weakness.*
(2 Corinthians 12:9)

God is well aware of the devices of the enemy.
He understands the spiritual warfare in which we
must often engage in order to secure our spiritual
stand. Therefore, throughout the Word of God,

He gives us the proper instructions on what to do when we are weak and how to lean on Him to become strong.

God is always listening when you speak. The devil tries to trick you into believing that because you have sinned, God does not want to hear anything you have to say. Countless numbers of people have put off serving God for years with the excuse, "I'll serve Him once I get myself together." If you wait until you feel worthy enough to serve God, then you will probably never serve Him.

What makes God so spectacular is that, despite His sovereignty, He reminds us,

> *For we do not have a High Priest who cannot sympathize with our weaknesses, but was in all points tempted as we are, yet without sin. Let us therefore come boldly to the throne of grace, that we may obtain mercy and find grace to help in time of need.* (Hebrews 4:15–16)

Several significant truths are revealed in these verses that extinguish the enemy's lies of condemnation. We should never feel there is anything we are experiencing that God does not understand or cannot give us a resolution for. Hebrews 4 tells us the following:

1. Christ Jesus was tempted *"in all points,"* just as we are tempted.

2. Although Jesus was tempted, He remained *"without sin."* Therefore, in Him, we hold the power to conquer our sinful nature and the things that have been keeping us bound. *"For if we have been united together in the likeness of His death, certainly we also shall be in the likeness of His resurrection, knowing this, that our old man was crucified with Him, that the body of sin might be done away with, that we should no longer be slaves of sin. For he who has died has been freed from sin"* (Romans 6:5–7).

3. If we do sin, the Lord does not cut off communication with us. Instead, He invites us to embrace His grace to find *"help in time of need."* First John 2:1 says, *"If anyone sins, we have an Advocate with the Father, Jesus Christ the righteous."*

Again, anytime you feel the need to stay away from God because of sin, it is because you have succumbed to the condemning lies of the devil. In the garden of Eden, the first thing Adam and Eve did after they had eaten the forbidden fruit was to hide from God. (See Genesis 3:6–10.) Today, people stay at home on Sunday mornings and refuse to come to church because they, also, are hiding from Him. Yet God knows everything. He knew that Adam and Eve had been conversing with the devil in the garden of Eden, and He knows when we "converse" with the devil, as well—by listening to his lies, allowing ourselves to be deceived by him, and following his suggestions.

Rather than casting us down when we fall, God restores us to Himself through the grace of salvation and forgiveness in Christ when we come to Him. God's grace not only restores us, but it also keeps us from sinning. Despite what you may be going through, if you run *to* God instead of *away* from Him, the burden of keeping from sinning will become less of a weight as you take upon yourself the yoke of Christ. Jesus said,

> God's grace not only restores us, but it also keeps us from sinning.

> *Come to Me, all you who labor and are heavy laden, and I will give you rest. Take My yoke upon you and learn from Me, for I am gentle and lowly in heart, and you will find rest for your souls. For My yoke is easy and My burden is light.*
> (Matthew 11:28–30)

Don't ever become so obsessed with what you cannot do that you forget to celebrate all that God has done for you. God is well aware of the enemy's hatred toward you, especially when you decide to serve Him with all your heart. The devil's hatred, however, is of no consequence compared to God's love for you. Those who are in a relationship with the Lord do not live their lives based upon fear and doubt. They understand that as they keep their commitment to remain faithful to Him, He will supply all their need *according to His riches in glory by Christ Jesus*" (Philippians 4:19).

You Can Prevail Over the Gates of Hell

Though the gates of hell are very real, you do not have to succumb to them. Hell's attacks do not prevail over those who know their God. Often, the hesitancy we feel about taking steps toward building a relationship with God comes from our awareness of the responsibility that accompanies it—the responsibility of living for Him and counteracting the work of the devil through spiritual warfare. Consequently, we unknowingly stagnate our own growth by shying away from the only One who holds the power to set us free from what has been holding us captive and limiting us.

The devil uses intimidation to keep you from activating the power that God has given you. He tells you that you cannot do certain things when God has said you can do all things through Christ

Jesus. (See Philippians 4:13.) He tries to convince you that you are weak and are no match for him and his attacks, when God has said, *"Therefore submit to God. Resist the devil and he will flee from you"* (James 4:7). He uses scare tactics and bullies you into thinking you are going to hell because of your hidden struggles, when God has said, *"My grace is sufficient for you, for My strength is made perfect in weakness"* (2 Corinthians 12:9). He pulls many people away from the church and defuses their potential spiritual power through Christ by deceiving them into believing in other gods, when God has said, *"You shall worship no other god"* (Exodus 34:14).

We must be aware of all the devil's tactics and subtle insinuations while remaining grounded in our relationship with God and the truth of His Word. In this way, we can counteract Satan's schemes and gain full victory over him.

6

DELIVERANCE FROM OUR FLESHLY NATURE

We have seen that there are literal gates of hell through which the unbelieving and unrepentant are led to an eternity of doom. Yet there are also other "gateways" that conduct people to hell. These are avenues of selfish, fleshly living that lead people to lifestyles of spiritual and physical destruction and ultimately to eternal punishment. Satan uses the *"lusts of our flesh [*"sinful nature" NIV*]"* (Ephesians 2:3) as a means of manipulating us, so that his voice becomes the prevailing influence in our lives, instead of God's voice. You cannot hear God when fleshly or carnal appetites control you.

The Scriptures outline many of the works of the flesh, born out of sinful desires:

Now the works of the flesh are evident, which are: adultery, fornication, uncleanness, lewdness, idolatry, sorcery, hatred, contentions, jealousies, outbursts of wrath, selfish ambitions, dissensions, heresies, envy, murders, drunkenness, revelries, and the like; of which I tell you beforehand, just as I also told you in time past, that those who practice such things will not inherit the kingdom of God. (Galatians 5:19–21)

The sinful nature controls those who do not know Christ. It can also be a snare for Christians. It is at war with the new nature of the Spirit, which believers receive at salvation. Paul wrote in Romans,

For I delight in the law of God according to the inward man. But I see another law in my members, warring against the law of my mind, and bringing me into captivity to the law of sin which is in my members. O wretched man that I am! Who will deliver me from this body of death? I thank God; through Jesus Christ our Lord! So then, with the mind I myself serve the law of God, but with the flesh the law of sin. There is therefore now no condemnation to those who are in Christ Jesus, who do not walk according to the flesh, but according to the Spirit. For the law of the Spirit of life in Christ Jesus has made me

free from the law of sin and death.
(Romans 7:22–8:2)

The remedy for living according to the sinful nature is this: *"Walk in the Spirit, and you shall not fulfill the lust of the flesh"* (Galatians 5:16). If we live and walk in the Spirit, we can overcome our sinful desires, shut these "gateways" that lead to destruction, and inherit the kingdom of God.

> *Those who live according to the flesh set their minds on the things of the flesh, but those who live according to the Spirit, the things of the Spirit. For to be carnally minded is death, but to be spiritually minded is life and peace. Because the carnal mind is enmity against God; for it is not subject to the law of God, nor indeed can be. So then, those who are in the flesh cannot please God....For if you live according to the flesh you will die; but if by the Spirit you put to death the deeds of the body, you will live. For as many as are led by the Spirit of God, these are sons of God.* (Romans 8:5–8, 13–14)

The sinful nature wants to fulfill fleshly desires, so we must do everything we can to overcome our sinful nature. Jesus said, *"If anyone desires to come after Me, let him deny himself, and take up his cross daily, and follow Me. For whoever desires to save his life will lose it, but whoever loses his life for My sake will save it"* (Luke 9:23–24). We must lay down earthly, ungodly desires and take up the cross of Christ daily. We must die daily to the works of the flesh in order to reign with Christ for eternity.

To *die daily* means that we must continually allow the will of God to become more prevalent in our lives than the desires of the flesh. This doesn't mean we won't have struggles and challenges. It simply means that because Christ has put all things under His feet, we have the power through Him to defeat every foe that attempts to annihilate us—including our sinful nature and the demonic forces that try to incite us to yield to it. Again, the gates of hell cannot prevail against you when you know who you are in Christ Jesus.

> We must lay down earthly desires and take up the cross of Christ daily.

THE DEVIL'S THREE TEMPTATIONS

In order to learn how to overcome the fleshly nature, let us begin by seeing how Jesus defeated temptation.

Then Jesus was led up by the Spirit into the wilderness to be tempted by the devil. And when He had fasted forty days and forty nights, afterward He was hungry. Now when the tempter came to Him, he said, "If You are the Son of God, command that these stones become bread." But He answered and said, "It is written, 'Man shall not live by bread alone, but by every word that proceeds from the mouth of God.'" Then the devil took Him up into the holy city, set Him on the pinnacle of the temple, and said to Him, "If You are the Son of God, throw Yourself down. For it is written: 'He shall give His angels charge over you,' and, 'In their hands they shall bear you up, lest you dash your foot against a stone.'" Jesus said to him, "It is written again, 'You shall not tempt the LORD your God.'" Again, the devil took Him up on an exceedingly high mountain, and showed Him all the kingdoms of the world and their glory. And he said to Him, "All these things I will give You if You will fall down and worship me." Then Jesus said to him, "Away with you, Satan! For it is written, 'You shall worship the LORD your God, and Him only you shall serve.'" Then the devil left Him, and behold, angels came and ministered to Him. (Matthew 4:1–11)

The devil used three main temptations against Jesus, and these are the same poisonous ingredients he uses to deceive us into ruining our lives today: (1) appetite, (2) recklessness or self-destruction, and (3) materialism or ill-gotten gain. Let us look generally at these three areas and then see how they play out more specifically in our lives.

The Temptation of the Appetite

The devil knew that after fasting for forty days, Jesus would be hungry. He used this opportunity to play on Jesus' basic physical needs to try to get Him to stop relying on His heavenly Father and to satisfy his hunger the devil's way. He tried to control Jesus by attempting to trick Him into taking matters into His own hands before the Father's angels could minister to Him.

You never want the devil to be the one you take advice from or obey, especially right after coming off a fast. At that time, your spirit is especially open to receive from the spiritual realm, and you do not want it to be contaminated by evil forces that seek its destruction. Instead of responding to your needs according to your fleshly appetites, live according to Jesus' example of self-control and trust in God. Jesus told Satan, *"It is written, 'Man shall not live by bread alone, but by every word that proceeds from the mouth of God'"* (Matthew 4:4).

The Temptation of Recklessness or Self-Destruction

Satan next tried trickery in an attempt to get Jesus to leap from a high pinnacle, saying that God would protect Him. Today, the devil continues to try to entice us to destroy ourselves, either by encouraging us to live reckless and lawless lifestyles, or by oppressing us to the point that we willingly take our own lives. Jesus thwarted this temptation by telling the devil, *"It is written again, 'You shall not tempt the LORD your God'"* (Matthew 4:7). We are not to live recklessly or dangerously, with the false belief that God will protect us no matter what we might do. Moreover, if we are oppressed and are tempted to be despondent or suicidal, we must hold on to our trust in God and His love.

> *Blessed be the God and Father of our Lord Jesus Christ, the Father of mercies and God of all comfort, who comforts us in all our tribulation, that we may be able to comfort those who are in any trouble, with the comfort with which we ourselves are comforted by God.* (2 Corinthians 1:3–4)

The Temptation of Materialism or Ill-Gotten Gain

Finally, the devil tried to bargain with Jesus over things that already belonged to Him through the Father. Satan said, in effect, "I will give you the whole world on one condition: fall down and worship me." Jesus made it clear to the devil that this was not a bargain He was willing to accept: *"Then Jesus said to him, 'Away with you, Satan! For it is written, "You shall worship the LORD your God, and Him only you shall serve"'"* (Matthew 4:10). Anytime you are offered power, influence, or wealth in exchange for your soul, realize that it is much too high a price to pay, and walk away.

> If you are telling someone about God's love, you don't want him to see you living a sinful life.

We must also remember that, in making decisions and choices about our behavior, what we do today has the potential to affect someone else for a lifetime. If you are telling someone about the love of God, you do not want this same person to see you acting out a sinful lifestyle. Often, the only picture of God an individual is able to see is the one you reflect through your actions. It is therefore not only for your own sake, but also for the sake of others, that you must keep yourself in a strong relationship with God and resist yielding to the desires of the sinful nature.

SNARES OF THE SINFUL NATURE

The temptations of fulfilling the desires of the appetites, living recklessly, and having worldly success at the cost of eternal life with God can be seen in many of the snares and destructive behavior people fall into today. Among these snares are sensualism, materialism, pride, and seeking escape and relief through ungodly indulgences. Why do people become ensnared by the sinful nature? Let us look at several "gateways" to hell we need to be watchful over.

The Gateway of Sensualism

One gateway to hell that pulls people away from their moral base is the lure of sensualism. Our senses are one of the most vulnerable areas of our lives, so the devil intrudes on them and tries to entice us into all types of ungodly behaviors. Satan knows what buttons to push to cause his desired reaction. In my visions of hell, I saw that demons laugh at those whom they have been able to entice. They laugh because they know that hell will be waiting for them, and it is a place of unrest; there is no love, joy, peace, or compassion there—only torment.

With the sexual revolution of the 1960s, the gateway to sexual degradation was clearly revealed, even though it has been in existence since the beginning of history. In the Bible, we see examples of sexual immorality in the people of Sodom and Gomorrah, whose misplaced passions cost them their existence, and in Amnon, David's son, who raped his own sister. (See Genesis 18:20–19:26; 2 Samuel 13:1–19.) Today, sexual immorality has increasingly become a way of life in our culture, rather than being recognized as an opposing force that we are to resist.

The deception of Satan is like a canker that begins its infestation with individuals, then spreads to annihilate entire communities. Jude, referencing Sodom and Gomorrah, wrote,

> *Sodom and Gomorrah, and the cities around them in a similar manner to these, having given themselves over to sexual immorality and gone after strange flesh, are set forth as an example, suffering the vengeance of eternal fire.* (Jude 7)

The people of these cities gave themselves over to self-indulgence. As Satan walked about seeking whom he could devour, they proved the perfect targets. They showed him no resistance and gave him no reason to flee. They were the perfect breeding ground for contention, vile acts, and lawlessness—attributes that he used to his benefit until, ultimately, they were all destroyed for their insolence.

The devil will use any means necessary to entrap nonbelievers and to distract believers from doing the work of the Lord. He presents what is appealing to the eyes, says things that tickle the ears, and entices us to satisfy the flesh with what God has forbidden us to touch.

What happened after the serpent beguiled Eve in the garden of Eden through her senses and her pride? *"When the woman saw that the tree was good for food, that it was* **pleasant to the eyes,** *and a tree* **desirable to make one wise,** *she took of its fruit and ate"* (Genesis 3:6, emphasis added). The devil played upon her senses to

> The devil will use any means necessary to distract believers from doing the Lord's work.

get her to indulge the appetites of her soul and body with something God had forbidden. Satan knows that if he can get you to see through his eyes and distract you long enough, he can eventually entice you into partaking of the very thing God has warned you to reject. Consider the following account from Bishop Bloomer:

Sometime ago, when I was away preaching, I was suddenly faced with a very unfamiliar temptation. I have never been one to watch pornography, even before I knew God and accepted Him as Lord and Savior. Nevertheless, during one of my speaking engagements to preach, I found myself in my hotel room clicking through the television channels when I heard my inner voice suggest to me to watch a "flick." I pressed the menu button and began scanning down the menu options. It was as if I was being overtaken by some force; at the same time, I was embarrassed, so I closed the curtains and locked the door. No one else was in the room with me, yet I still knew in my heart that this was wrong. To ensure that what I was about to do would remain "my secret," I called the room of my attendants to make sure that they would not be returning to my room. By then, the gate was wide open. I was moments away from entering the world of pornography and had no idea what was drawing me there. The channel menu came up with thirty different pornographic titles from which to choose: *Naughty House Wives*, *Girls Just Want to Have Fun*, *Lesbian Lovers*, *Two Guys and a Girl*. Still, none of these titles struck my interest. Just when I was about to give up, I saw it—*Sexual Chocolate*—and I thought, *I like chocolate.* The preview popped up...$39.99. When I saw this price, the gate immediately closed. Maybe it's because I'm frugal, but I could not see myself paying forty dollars for something such as this.

As I began to snap out of this daze, I decided to find out what was going on in the hotel. I called down to the front desk and asked, "What type of convention did you have in the hotel recently?" The front desk clerk answered, "Yesterday was the last day of the Gay Convention."

> **God knows how to get our attention long enough to show us a way of escape.**

Finally, it dawned on me! The residue was still in that room. Had I not been a person disciplined with my money, I most certainly would have opened the door to a series of pitfalls by pressing that button on the menu and entering into the damaging world of pornography.

God knows how to get our attention long enough to show us a way of escape.

Curses do not come without a cause. There is a reason for what we go through. It is not always our fault that the curse exists. Sometimes it is a generational ailment that has been permitted to fester for years without anyone taking authority over it and ceasing its existence. Still, there is definitely something that we can do to destroy it and keep it from taking over our lives. (See, for example, Psalm 50:15; James 4:7.)

Sensualism can create a false sense of reality. For instance, two people of the same sex who decide to come together in an intimate relationship still must resort to God's original plan in order to have a child. The egg of a woman must be fertilized by the sperm of a man in order to replenish the earth with children. Unfortunately, many people tend to use God's plans only when it is convenient for them. Afterward, they usually resort to their own way of doing things, even when it goes against the commandments of God and perverts God's truth. We read in Romans,

Although they knew God, they did not glorify Him as God, nor were thankful, but became futile in their thoughts, and their foolish hearts were darkened.

(Romans 1:21)

When the heart is darkened, it engages in its own truth, regardless of who it hurts or damages along the way.

Professing to be wise, they became fools, and changed the glory of the incorruptible God into an image made like corruptible man; and birds and four-footed animals and creeping things. (Romans 1:22–23)

When you begin creating your own truth, you ultimately create your own idols. You no longer rely on God for your provision but instead create prefabricated illusions as a means of fulfillment.

Therefore God also gave them up to uncleanness, in the lusts of their hearts, to dishonor their bodies among themselves.
(v. 24)

God created the senses, and when they are used in the proper way, they are wonderful gifts that enable us to enjoy the world God has created and to exercise dominion over it. Yet we must be on guard against sensualistic desires and pitfalls. Temptation is real, and it is a trick of the enemy. When you feel tempted to engage in ungodly and immoral acts, take time to call upon the strength of God to pull you through it. You may need to ask a strong believer to agree with you in prayer to stand against the temptation. Rebuke the devil in the name of Jesus, pray the blood of Jesus over your life, seek God diligently, and fill the atmosphere of your life with a spirit of praise.

The Gateway of Materialism

Another gateway to hell is materialism. While material goods, in themselves, are not evil or wrong, an overemphasis on them can be spiritually deadly:

> *For we brought nothing into this world, and it is certain we can carry nothing out. And having food and clothing, with these we shall be content. But those who desire to be rich fall into temptation and a snare, and into many foolish and harmful lusts which drown men in destruction and perdition. For the love of money is a root of all kinds of evil, for which some have strayed from the faith in their greediness, and pierced themselves through with many sorrows. But you, O man of God, flee these things and pursue righteousness, godliness, faith, love, patience, gentleness. Fight the good fight of faith, lay hold on eternal life, to which you were also called and have confessed the good confession in the presence of many witnesses.* (1 Timothy 6:7–12)

God often provides for us through material goods, and our dominion over the world includes the stewardship of physical resources. There are practical, everyday activities and pursuits involving material goods we must engage in to support our families and maintain our homes. We deal with the material world in order bring about certain dreams and aspirations, which involve jobs, careers, businesses, and so forth. God wants us to enjoy His gifts to us, and we may be blessed

> **God is the Giver of all good things, and we must follow His leading in all we do.**

materially. Yet Satan wants to take away our God-given dominion by enticing us with materialism and other lusts. We must therefore never lose sight of the fact that God is the Giver of all good things, and we must follow His leading in all we do.

> *And whatever you do in word or deed, do all in the name of the Lord Jesus, giving thanks to God the Father through Him.*
> (Colossians 3:17)

> *Do not be deceived, my beloved brethren. Every good gift and every perfect gift is from above, and comes down from the Father of lights, with whom there is no*

variation or shadow of turning. Of His own will He brought us forth by the word of truth, that we might be a kind of firstfruits of His creatures. (James 1:16–18)

Unfortunately, we often work tirelessly to obtain our desires, and then we ask God to bless them, instead of consulting Him first. Your number one priority as you seek to fulfill your goals and aspirations under God's guidance should be to inspire others by your actions so that they can clearly see the Spirit of God resonating from your character.

Moreover, even though we may acquire earthly riches and material gain, we still need God's divine wisdom and guidance to attain all the things He has supplied for us according to His good pleasure.

*And my God shall supply all your need according to **His riches in glory** by Christ Jesus.*
(Philippians 4:19, emphasis added)

The book of Luke gives a very descriptive parable regarding the fate of a certain rich man who was more concerned with his riches than with heeding the Word of the Lord.

There was a certain rich man who was clothed in purple and fine linen and fared sumptuously every day. But there was a certain beggar named Lazarus, full of sores, who was laid at his gate....

(Luke 16:19–20)

Again, you cannot judge the true nature of a person's spiritual level and godly authority by his or her outward appearance.

...desiring to be fed with the crumbs which fell from the rich man's table. Moreover the dogs came and licked his sores. So it was that the beggar died, and was carried by the angels to Abraham's bosom. The rich man also died and was buried. And being in torments in Hades, he lifted up his eyes and saw Abraham afar off, and Lazarus in his bosom.

(vv. 21–23)

Unfortunately, many on earth are consumed by a lust for material goods. It is not until they get to hell that they awaken to see the full scope of their spiritual deception.

Then [the rich man] *cried and said, "Father Abraham, have mercy on me, and send Lazarus that he may dip the tip of his finger in water and cool my tongue; for I am tormented in this flame." But Abraham said, "Son, remember that in your*

lifetime you received your good things, and likewise Lazarus evil things; but now he is comforted and you are tormented."
(Luke 16:24–25)

When the rich man realized there was no way out, he begged Abraham to send Lazarus back to the earth to warn his brothers to heed the Word of the Lord so they would not succumb to the same fate. Abraham reminded the rich man that if his brothers would not listen to Moses and the prophets of God, neither would they listen to one who rose from the dead. (See verses 27–31.) God has sent people throughout the earth to spread the good news of the gospel of Jesus Christ. It is up to those who hear the Word to take heed as God speaks through those whom He has strategically placed in their paths.

> **Never think you have so much in life that you no longer need God.**

We are never to become so obsessed with material gain that we trade our eternal souls for it! *"For what will it profit a man if he gains the whole world, and loses his own soul?"* (Mark 8:36). Never think that you have so much in life that you no longer need God. As we saw in the previous chapter, we are to seek God first, and everything else we need will be supplied. *"But seek first the kingdom of God and His righteousness, and all these things shall be added to you"* (Matthew 6:33).

You can become so consumed with the cares of this world that you no longer desire to hear what God has to say about the world and its false promises. This is a very dangerous mind-set to embrace. The devil's trick is to cause your mind to become so inundated by the pursuit of wealth and materialism that the fear of *not* having these things takes precedence over your pursuit of the kingdom of God. The rich man in the parable from Luke 16 had become so intoxicated with securing his wealth that he had no time to give to God. By the time he realized the consequences of his error, it was too late.

Material riches mean nothing without God. I am sure that the rich man would gladly have traded all his riches for one more chance to repent, serve God, and help the poor. This does not mean that God expects us to live a life of poverty, but that we are to acknowledge Him in all our ways. Even if we are prosperous, we are not to turn our backs on God and refuse to hear what He has to say. We are instead to reflect His abundantly generous and giving nature. When you receive Jesus as Lord of your life and obey His commands, you will prosper in a way that causes God to remember you in both life and death.

You do not have to be wealthy to become caught up in materialism, relying on earthly resources rather than God's provision. If you do not trust God to provide for you, you can fall into the devil's trap. We read in Numbers 13 that God had already promised the children of Israel the land of Canaan before He commanded Moses to send men to spy out the land. When the spies reported to the people, instead of rejoicing over the abundance in the Promised Land, the majority of them gave a negative assessment of it and, as a result, planted fear and doubt in the minds of the Israelites.

> **If you rely on earthly resources rather than God's provision, you can fall into the devil's trap.**

It is vital to trust in God's provision, in His way. You do not have to live in misery and strife, seeking after things of the earth, when God has already promised that if you trust in His provision, you will have all you need. Apply your faith, and simply receive.

Bring all the tithes into the storehouse, that there may be food in My house, and try Me now in this," says the LORD of hosts, "If I will not open for you the windows of

*heaven and pour out for you such bless-
ing that there will not be room enough to
receive it."* (Malachi 3:10)

*Do not worry, saying, "What shall we
eat?" or "What shall we drink?" or "What
shall we wear?" For after all these things
the Gentiles seek. For your heavenly Father knows that you need all these things.
But seek first the kingdom of God and His
righteousness, and all these things shall
be added to you.* (Matthew 6:31–33)

All the spies except Joshua and Caleb said,

*We went to the land where you sent us. It
truly flows with milk and honey, and this
is its fruit. **Nevertheless**....*
(Numbers 13:27–28, emphasis added)

When God makes a promise to you, never use
the word *nevertheless* to sum up His blessings.
The spies became overwhelmed by the thought of
the walled cities and the strength of the people:
*"Nevertheless the people who dwell in the land
are strong; the cities are fortified and very large"*
(v. 28). They forgot about the fact that God had
already given them the land. All they needed to
do was to follow the Lord's instructions and walk
into what He had already promised was theirs.

Instead, they felt they had to rely on their own resources, which weren't sufficient.

You have to be able to distinguish between the voice of God and the lies and enticements of the devil. Hear as God hears, and see as He sees. When God says that eternal life is yours, believe Him. Likewise, when He says He has given you dominion over the earth and that He will supply all your needs, believe Him and do not allow contrary voices from Satan's kingdom to persuade you to be filled with doubt and unbelief.

The Gateway of Pride and Self-Sufficiency

A third gateway is one of intellectual pride and religious self-sufficiency. As we discussed earlier, many people today are buying into all types of false ideologies and philosophies. These subtle demonic doctrines teach us to live without God and to look only to ourselves for absolutely everything we need. Satan's pride and desire to rise above the One who created him, in order to live for himself according to his own standards, caused him to fall from glory. He entices us to give in to the same temptations, as he did with Adam and Eve.

Satan has been upon the earth for many years promoting his product called "Create Your Own Truth" or "There Is No Absolute Truth." This doctrine says, "Reject the life God has designed for you to fulfill and instead create your own *cosmos*." The more we accept this doctrine, the more we allow ourselves to become engulfed in deception that leads to ungodliness, immorality, and more falsehood. Satan always sprinkles enough truth on his poison to get you to swallow it. He says what you want to hear and what makes you feel good for the moment. Yet rest assured that beneath the surface, there is an unstable foundation just waiting to crumble under his lie, burying you with it.

A very clear account of the depths of Satan's deception is outlined in the book of Jude:

> *And the angels which kept not their first estate* ["proper domain" NKJV], *but left their own habitation, he hath reserved in everlasting chains under darkness unto the judgment of the great day.* (Jude 6 KJV)

These angels had everything they needed in their *"first estate"*—until Satan came along and deceived them. Their original estate consisted of the presence of God and His miraculous works and craftsmanship. It was an estate handed to them by the King Himself—worth more than silver or gold. Yet they left this habitation in exchange for deceitfulness and death.

How were they so easily deceived by the devices of Satan? They simply took time to listen to what the devil had to say. They voluntarily allowed Satan's lies to enter into their ear-gates and then into their wills. So they also succumbed to the same fate as the devil—becoming bankrupt in the things of God, evicted from His habitation, and under His condemnation. It is the devil's agenda to spread his ungodly doctrine so that we fall prey to the same fate as he and the fallen angels.

A passage from Isaiah 14 allows us to see how Satan boasted of his rebellious and ill-fated agenda:

> *For you have said in your heart: "I will ascend into heaven, I will exalt my throne above the stars of God; I will also sit on the mount of the congregation on the farthest sides of the north; I will ascend above the heights of the clouds, I will be like the Most High." Yet you shall be brought down to Sheol, to the lowest depths of the Pit.*
> (Isaiah 14:13–15)

Instead of accomplishing the impossible and unimaginable feat of becoming like the Most High, Satan was defeated by God. He was made a public disgrace and was brought down to hell.

Never allow the devil into your ear-gates; do not let him estrange you from the place that God has established for your existence. Your inheritance is an estate from the Father filled with everything that you will ever need in life: *"And my God shall supply all your need according to His riches in glory by Christ Jesus"* (Philippians 4:19). There is no need to go searching anywhere else. Everything that you need has already been supplied to you in Christ. You should never allow anything that you hear to dissuade you from God's truth.

If you subscribe to the false doctrine of "create your own truth" that is currently circulating in our culture, then this will be a very dangerous place for your existence. Truth can be discovered only by seeking God's Word. It is through the Word of God that you will learn His ways and will for your life.

> **Your inheritance from the Father is filled with everything you will need in life.**

Paul wrote to the Galatians,

> *There are some who trouble you and want to pervert the gospel of Christ. But even if we, or an angel from heaven, preach any other gospel to you than what we have*

preached to you, let him be accursed.
(Galatians 1:7–8)

Our eternal salvation depends on knowing and following the true gospel of Christ. We must be very clear concerning in whom we believe and what we believe.

The gospel of Jesus Christ does not come to tickle the ears of people; it is given in order to reveal God's truth. *"You shall know the truth, and the truth shall make you free"* (John 8:32). The truth makes you free by exposing the lies of Satan. There is no truth in the devil (see verse 44), and he would like to create a false image of truth in your mind that you spend the rest of your life needlessly trying to fulfill.

Yet the gates of hell will not prevail against the principles of God's Word. Seek God's ways and learn His Word in order to discover and put these principles into practice. We have a firm promise from Jesus Christ that if we remain grounded on the foundation He has set forth for us to follow, the enemy will not gain the victory over us.

The Gateway of Ungodly Indulgences

Another gateway to hell is that of seeking escape and relief in life through ungodly indulgences. We have seen that when we go through very difficult times, the enemy often uses our vulnerabilities against us. Instead of turning to God during these times, we can be tempted to seek comfort through such things as unhealthy relationships and substance abuse. Sometimes, we seek these things as a means of self-medication when the problem can only be truly resolved through divine intervention and a change in lifestyle.

The danger of alcohol and drugs is that they can be life-altering substances. Drinking to excess, for instance, clouds people's minds and can cause them to make bad decisions or to unveil secrets that should remain confidential. Because its effect is impaired judgment, it uproots self-control, rendering its victims susceptible to even further humiliation and danger due to a lack of awareness. Countless stories are told of individuals who compromised their principles and were lured into sexual immorality while under the influence of alcohol.

The influence of alcohol has no consideration for the well-being of loved ones, friends, or other innocent victims. Once it activates its effects on the one who is drinking, it can spill over into the lives of everyone who is associated with the person.

How can so many people overlook the danger of such a mind-altering and debilitating gateway such as alcohol? The statistics regarding its devastating effects on humanity are staggering, yet alcohol abuse is still not perceived as a serious threat to society. Consider this data for the United States:

- Alcohol abuse wastes an estimated $184.6 billion per year in health care, business, and criminal justice costs.
- Alcohol abuse causes about 75,000 deaths per year.
- In 1997, 40 percent of convicted rape and sexual assault offenders said they were drinking at the time of their crime.
- In 2002, more than 70,000 students between the ages of 18 and 24 were victims of alcohol-related sexual assault or date rape.
- Alcohol played a role in 28 percent of suicides in children ages 9 to 15.
- An estimated 480,000 children are mistreated each year by a caretaker with alcohol problems.[1]

Satan would love to keep your mind impaired rather than soberly watching for his attacks (see Titus 2:11–13), and alcohol is one of his "portals" to unhappiness upon the earth. Unfortunately, even in the church, people use certain Scriptures to justify engaging in excessive consumption of alcohol, such as *"No longer drink only water, but use a little wine for your stomach's sake and your frequent infirmities"* (1 Timothy 5:23). Yet anything done in recreation that has the potency to alter a person's behavior in a way that causes him to lose control of his senses should be something from which a person should consider disciplining himself.

The real danger of indulging in substance abuse is that people may forsake their relationship with the living God. There are backsliders in hell who once served the Lord, but then returned to the bondage of their old lifestyles. I know many people, for instance, who had a drink-

> The danger of substance abuse is that people may forsake their relationship with God.

ing problem. They were saved and delivered for a while, but the day came when the tempter enticed them to go with their buddies to get drunk. At that moment of enticement, when they were lured into temptation, many of them were involved in accidents. They wound up being arrested, losing their jobs, or even being sent to prison.

In such situations, people are tempted to feel like failures and to give up their faith. Meanwhile, the devil sits back and laughs because he feels that his mission toward them has been accomplished.

There is a lying spirit in the land, telling you that you cannot overcome bondages such as substance abuse. The spirit of religion tells you that once you have committed an offence, you are doomed for hell. This is not true. You can overcome, and God is still reaching out to you. The Man called Jesus, who shed His blood on your behalf, has more power to deliver you from drinking, adultery, fornication, lying, and all the sins of your flesh than you could ever imagine. "[Jesus] *is also able to save to the uttermost those who come to God through Him, since He always lives to make intercession for them"* (Hebrews 7:25).

Regardless of what we go through in life, we can still be saved through Jesus Christ. He did not come to condemn you—a fact that He so eloquently confirmed in John 3:17: *"God did not send His Son into the world to condemn the world, but that the world through Him might be saved."* He did not come to destroy you; He came to give you life, and to give it to you more abundantly. (See John 10:10.) That is the truth of God's Word. The Son of God did not come into the world to point out our wrongdoings or to condemn us. He came to reveal that eternal life is available to all who will receive it, all who will repent and embrace Jesus Christ as Lord and Savior.

We must recognize that when we are faced with adversity, the devil will tempt us to resort to ungodly means of having our needs met. Instead of inclining our ears to God for understanding and knowledge, we are often quick to listen to the advice of those who lack divine revelation about our lives and circumstances. We must stop focusing so much upon what we see with our natural eyes and allow the Spirit of God to reveal what is truly going on behind the scenes spiritually.

God counteracts what we see in the natural with the comforting words of 2 Corinthians 5:7: *"For we walk by faith, not by sight."* Often, it's the complexity of our lives and our lack of understanding about it that land us in trouble. Our confusion can be unraveled in an instant by replacing it with the voice and wisdom of God. If we give our ears to the wisdom of God, He promises to give us understanding.

Be still, and know that I am God.
(Psalm 46:10)

Incline your ear to wisdom, and apply your heart to understanding. (Proverbs 2:2)

If any of you lacks wisdom, let him ask of God, who gives to all liberally and without reproach, and it will be given to him.

(James 1:5)

There is absolutely no struggle that you are experiencing that God does not understand. And there is nothing that affects you in life, whether physically, mentally, or emotionally, that God cannot give you divine revelation about how to overcome. He is very familiar with our plight, and He reminds us of this in Hebrews 4:15: *"For we do not have a High Priest who cannot sympathize with our weaknesses, but was in all points tempted as we are, yet without sin."*

> **There is absolutely no struggle you can experience that God does not understand.**

We do not need to turn to ungodly indulgences to relieve our fear and pain. Whether we are affected by what we see, hear, smell, taste, or touch, God has already provided a way of escape for us. (See 1 Corinthians 10:13.) He knows what to do to resolve any conflict that attempts to hinder us from developing a proper relationship with Him. *"[God] is able to do exceedingly abundantly above all that we ask or think, according to the power that works in us"* (Ephesians 3:20).

Anything you can think or imagine, God is able to exceed.

OVERCOMING TEMPTATION AND THE SINFUL NATURE

The devil not only wants to destroy your confession of faith, but he also wants to destroy *you*—both in life and in death. As we have seen, he uses people's uncontrolled fleshly nature as one of his avenues of destruction.

Giving in to the sins of the flesh can destroy us physically and spiritually. Yet, regardless of how strong a grip the enemy seems to have on you, you can be released from it in the name of Jesus. In my walk with Christ, I have learned that if we are honest and true with God regarding our struggles, His mercy reigns in us. *"God is Spirit, and those who worship Him must worship in spirit and truth"* (John 4:24).

The apostle Peter wrote, *"Be sober, be vigilant; because your adversary the devil walks about like a roaring lion, seeking whom he may devour"* (1 Peter 5:8). Never allow yourself to be an easy target for the devil. This means that you should never become so intoxicated by your natural environment that you begin to neglect the spiritual warfare that is needed to secure your spiritual stand with God. Satan knows that he cannot just destroy you at will. Rather, he must walk about and seek the perfect opportunity in which to devour you. If you remain vigilant in your spiritual stand with God, however, when the devil walks about seeking this opportunity, it will not be found in you. Instead, he will walk past you time and time again, wanting to possess you, oppress you, and even kill you, but the power of God that resides within you will present him with a sign that reads OFF LIMITS!

Sometimes, it takes time to grow up spiritually and learn to live and walk by the Spirit rather than by the sinful nature. Temptation is real and demonic powers are real. This is why God often brings people into our lives to pray for us and help us overcome situations that are holding us in captivity. We need to support one another in order to thwart the attacks of the enemy and overcome the lusts of the sinful nature.

> **What is standing between you and God?**

What is currently standing between you and God? Is it a vicious or all-consuming pursuit of wealth, idolizing your job, bad relationships, sensualism, feelings of condemnation, addiction, a negative mind-set, pride, or self-sufficiency?

Whatever it is, you should not postpone being reconciled with God because of it. Remember that when Jesus ended His forty-day fast, the devil did everything within his power to try to pull Him away from His relationship with the Father, and this is the same tactic the devil uses today. He presents everything that he can possibly think of to feed our fleshly appetites and keep us distracted from God and His ways. He will promise you the world—in exchange for your soul.

People who live to please their sinful nature cannot inherit the kingdom of God and face eternal punishment. Individuals in hell see the results of their earthly indulgences. The lies they believed begin to unravel and reveal the depths of their deception.

Seducing lies, such as "There is no hell...don't fear God...do what makes you feel good....God understands" are straight from the pit of hell. These lies undermine your reverence for God, convincing you to reject Him and ignore His coming judgment. The devil makes sure that those who are vulnerable to his voice enjoy the lusts of their flesh more than the commandments of God. This is why I weep and cry for souls—and pray they will heed the Word of the Lord:

Reckon yourselves to be dead indeed to sin, but alive to God in Christ Jesus our

Lord. Therefore do not let sin reign in your mortal body, that you should obey it in its lusts. And do not present your members as instruments of unrighteousness to sin, but present yourselves to God as being alive from the dead, and your members as instruments of righteousness to God. For sin shall not have dominion over you, for you are not under law but under grace.

(Romans 6:11–14)

Why should you serve the temporal and corrupt desires of the flesh while you are on the earth and then die and go to hell forever? Think about what you're doing. Change your mind and way of life now by turning to the living God, who is begging you to stop living according to your sinful nature. Believe what the Spirit is saying to the churches: "Repent, My people, and turn to the living God. He will wash you clean."

God Will Never Forsake Us

There are many pitfalls in regard to the sinful nature. Each of us has issues, but God has given us the power to overcome them. This is what the gospel is all about. You must understand that if you fall, God is more than able to pick you up and to show you His love, just as a parent shows love toward a baby. When you have a newborn baby, you love, protect, and watch over her, and as that baby grows, you are attentive as she learns to crawl and walk. When she stumbles, bumps her head, and begins to cry, you bring her close and comfort her.

Likewise, God will never leave you or forsake you. (See Hebrews 13:5.) Regardless of the circumstances, He is committed to your well-being when you earnestly seek Him for deliverance. The many visions I have had are a true testament to His power and determination to see us through whatever challenges we face.

---

[1] Alcohol statistics were derived from the following sources: "Updating Estimates of the Economic Costs of Alcohol Abuse in the United States: Estimates, Update Methods, and Data," U.S. Department of Health and Human Services, December 2000 <http://pubs.niaaa.nih.gov/publications/economic-2000/alcoholcost.PDF> July 10, 2007; <http://www.msnbc.msn.com/id/6089353> July 10, 2007; "Alcohol, Crime, and the Criminal Justice System," L. Greenfield and M. Henneberg, "Alcohol and Crime: Research and Practice for Prevention," Alcohol Policy XII Conference: Washington, DC, 11–14 June 2000; <http://www.niaaa.nih.gov/AboutNIAAA/AdvisoryCouncil/CouncilMinutes/min4-02.htm> July 10, 2007; Tegan A. Culler, "The Poison Within," *Children's Voice,* a publication of Child Welfare League of America, November/December 2003 <http://www.cwla.org/articles/cv0311poison.htm> July 10, 2007; *Collaboration, Coordination and Cooperation: Helping Children Affected by Parental Addiction and Family Violence* (New York: Children of Alcoholics Foundation, Inc.,) 1996.

7

DELIVERANCE THROUGH SPIRITUAL WARFARE

In the last chapter, we saw how important it is to live by the Spirit and not to let the sinful nature take control of our lives. Keeping a rein on the sinful nature not only preserves our stand with God, but it also enables us to be spiritually alert and prepared for spiritual warfare.

As we have seen in previous chapters, we are fighting against demonic forces whose assignment is to destroy us. In my visions, I have seen armies of demons in hell. Just as armed forces upon the earth have different levels and ranks, there are also ranks among these demonic militant forces. They have lieutenants, corporals, and privates. I saw many of them standing at attention, awaiting their orders. They had fangs and broken wings, and a horrendous odor came from them. They also had the power to change their forms.

I also saw many demons and evil forces in an arena-like area in hell. Some of them had teeth. Some of them had hair. Some of them had tails like monkeys, and others were as large as bears. A few of the demons were about twelve feet tall and were shaped like vipers with large fangs protruding from their mouths. They would scream at each other. In front of them would stand an even bigger, more powerful demon holding a slate. He would be giving the smaller demons orders. There were also demons that would take orders from Satan himself and cause chaos in the lives of people and in places upon the earth.

> We need to bind demons to cancel their assignments and keep them from coming upon the earth.

When I saw these things, I heard the voice of the Lord remind me, "Whatever you bind on earth is bound in heaven. Whatever you loose on earth is loosed in heaven." (See Matthew 16:19; 18:18.) I thought, *We need to bind these demons to keep them from coming upon the earth, and to cancel their assignments.*

In order to bind evil forces through spiritual warfare, we must keep the following essential guidelines in mind.

LIVE IN THE AUTHORITY CHRIST GAVE YOU

First, we must live in the authority that Christ has given us. Jesus allowed Himself to be tortured and to die on the cross in order to gain victory over the devil and to give us access to His authority on earth. Mark 16 reveals the power and authority of the believer in Jesus' name, including the believer's authority over the forces of darkness.

> *He who believes and is baptized will be saved; but he who does not believe will be condemned. And these signs will follow those who believe: In My name they will cast out demons; they will speak with new tongues; they will take up serpents; and if they drink anything deadly, it will by no means hurt them; they will lay hands on the sick, and they will recover.*
>
> (Mark 16:16–18)

Those who believe in the Lord Jesus Christ…

- receive eternal salvation.

- have Jesus' authority to cast out demons.

- become filled with the Holy Spirit and can speak in heavenly languages *("new tongues")* in order to communicate with God and intercede for others.

- are endowed with the ability to overcome attacks that cause others to succumb to sickness or death.
- are the instruments of healing.

Jesus instructed His disciples, *"Heal the sick, cleanse the lepers, raise the dead, cast out demons. Freely you have received, freely give"* (Matthew 10:8). With the authority we have been given in the name of Jesus, we are to freely give the gift of deliverance to those who are bound by Satan. The devil hates the name of Jesus Christ, and he hates it when we call upon Jesus' name for deliverance because he knows he will be defeated. We must be submitted to God and believe without a doubt that Jesus is real and has all authority in heaven and on earth if we are to effectively wage spiritual warfare.

DEVELOP COMPASSION FOR THOSE BOUND BY SATAN

Second, we must have God's heart of compassion for those who are oppressed by the enemy. We read in the Scriptures,

> *The LORD is gracious and full of compassion, slow to anger and great in mercy. The LORD is good to all, and His tender mercies are over all His works.* (Psalm 145:8–9)

When evening had come, they brought to [Jesus] many who were demon-possessed. And He cast out the spirits with a word, and healed all who were sick, that it might be fulfilled which was spoken by Isaiah the prophet, saying: "He Himself took our infirmities and bore our sicknesses."
(Matthew 8:16–17)

When [Jesus] got into the boat, he who had been demon-possessed begged Him that he might be with Him. However, Jesus did not permit him, but said to him, "Go home to your friends, and tell them what great things the Lord has done for you, and how He has had compassion on you."
(Mark 5:18–19)

The Lord is deeply concerned for those who are bound, and we need to have the same compassion for them to set them free in His power. If we have no compassion and do nothing to help others, what are we going to do when we stand before the Lord and He asks, "Where are the souls you helped bring to salvation? Where are those you set free from Satan's oppression in My name? Where are those who were afflicted by sickness, and for whom you prayed to be healed?" You cannot say, "Lord, I was afraid to talk to people about you" or

"I didn't have time" or "I didn't really care about the welfare of others." God gives us gifts and fills us with His holy power to draw others to Him and to set them free from what binds them.

As ambassadors of Christ, we must carry the bloodstained cross and reveal Christ's sacrifice on behalf of the world and His desire to set people free. The church is to spread the Word of God and to reveal the love of Christ. Moreover, we should never allow the warfare that we face to prevent us from spreading the good news of the gospel. For example, one of the enemy's targets is our finances. A demonic stronghold may come against our financial stability in order to hinder us from spreading the Word to those who are destitute. We must stand against this stronghold and continue to reach out to those who are in need.

> God gives us gifts and fills us with His holy power to draw others to Him.

God wants you to be aware of demonic, seducing powers from hell that are working on the earth and how they try to control people to get them to succumb to their suggestions. As I mentioned in the previous chapter, demons will prey on people's vulnerability. Demonic deception causes people to do things they would not ordinarily do under clarity of mind. Two areas of attack I have encountered are depression and suicidal thoughts. We must know how to address these attacks in order to minister to others, as well as ourselves.

Compassion for Those Suffering from Depression

People often develop depression as a result of hurts, rejection, sorrow, and grief. Jesus knows the pain of these emotions and the impairment it can have upon people's minds. He Himself suffered the pain of rejection and grief, but He overcame any temptation to succumb to depression. He took our griefs and sorrows, bearing them for us on the cross.

> *He is despised and rejected by men, a Man of sorrows and acquainted with grief. And we hid, as it were, our faces from Him; He was despised, and we did not esteem Him. Surely He has borne our griefs and carried our sorrows.* (Isaiah 53:3–4)

You have to rebuke depression in Jesus' name and believe that God will deliver you. Sometimes, you may need to call upon the faith of another strong believer to stand with you in prayer to defeat this demonic hold upon the mind. Don't allow the enemy to bring depression upon you. Over the years, I have prayed to the Lord to set people free, and I have actually witnessed the power of God shake them like a leaf as they were freed. Then I have asked God to rebuild and restore their minds.

Compassion for Those with Suicidal Thoughts

Suicide demons come out of hell and crouch on the shoulders of people whispering lies: "Kill yourself...nobody loves you...nobody cares about you." I will never forget one day when I was ministering in a service in Chicago, and the Holy Spirit showed me the manic-depressive demon. A young man came up to me and said, "I've blasphemed the Holy Spirit."

I looked at him and thought to myself, *He can't even be thirty years old yet. I wonder how long he's been saved and what he's talking about.* I had already preached the Word of God, and I had begun praying for people. So the Lord told me, "Listen to him again."

The young man spoke again and said, "Will you pray for me that I don't go to hell? I'm really headed there because I blasphemed the Holy Spirit." Immediately, the Holy Spirit gave me wisdom to ask him how old he was when he was born again. He answered, "Just a couple of years ago."

"Well, how old were you when you blasphemed the Holy Spirit?"

He responded, "I was twelve years old."

I asked, "Honey, how could you have blasphemed the Holy Spirit if you didn't know Him?" I went on to explain, "In our earth today, many people curse and swear and do all types of wicked things before they become born again. After they accept Christ, sometimes they need help in being delivered and sometimes the Lord will just deliver them from these foul powers. The Lord really loves you, and I don't understand how you could have blasphemed Him at twelve years of age when you have only been saved for two years."

> **After being born again, some people still need help being delivered.**

The young man began to talk to me and explain some circumstances in his life, when all at once my eyes were opened to the spiritual realm, and I saw something green sitting on his head. It was shaped like a round object with four arms on one side and four arms on the other side. I remember noticing that it had eyes that were peering back at me. I just shook my head and prayed in my heart, "Jesus, what is that?"

The Lord answered, "It's a manic-depression demon. This thing has been on him since he was twelve years old. It has lied to him, seduced him, and told him all kinds of things that aren't true."

I looked again and saw four angels standing around him. One had a chain, one had a sword, one had the Bible, and one had a scroll. The Lord then revealed to me, "I'm going to deliver this man tonight. You're going to see Me deliver him to encourage the people."

I have learned that nearly everything that happens to me is to encourage God's people. So I asked this young man to pray the "Sinner's Prayer" with me for repentance and for recommitting himself to God. I prayed for him, and again I saw this evil being sitting on top of his head. It had a mouth and it was snarling at me. Its hands were extremely skinny, and it had one finger around the man's forehead, one around his eyes, one around his mouth, and one around his neck.

The Lord told me to loose this man from this manic-depression spirit in Jesus' name. I began to pray, "In the name of Jesus, you foul power of manic depression, I command you to loose this young man in the name of Jesus!" As I commanded this evil force to loose him, the young man began to shake up and down. One of the angels pried loose those four hands of the manic depression demon. As he pulled them off, another angel wrapped a chain around the demon, and I saw a Scripture written out:

> *Whatsoever thou shalt bind on earth shall be bound in heaven: and whatsoever thou shalt loose on earth shall be loosed in heaven.* (Matthew 16:19 KJV)

As I continued commanding that evil demon to loose the man and to be cast into the "dry places" in the name of Jesus (see Matthew 12:43; Luke 11:24), the angels began to take it away. The man then fell down on the floor, shaking and trembling. The Lord told me to pray for his restoration, due to the damage the demon had done to him. I prayed in the name of Jesus, as the Lord led me. Moments later, the man got up from the floor shaking his head. His eyes were so clear and beautiful when he finally said, "I feel good. I feel like something has lifted from my head."

"Son, it sure did," I responded. "God delivered you from that manic-depression demon." I began to pray for the restoration of his brain and his soul, in the name of Jesus, and I exercised faith that God would make him whole.

STAND STRONG DURING DEMONIC ATTACKS

Finally, we need to stay strong during demonic attacks and show others how they can do this, as well. There are many people in the world who are distressed and do not know what to do or how to be set free from the devil's assaults. In his play, *A Demon in My Bedroom*, Bishop Bloomer dramatically reveals the real-life encounter with evil spirits that numerous people experience. Likewise, many people call me and write me letters, pleading, "Mary, please tell me what this is. I hear these voices at night and I feel them pulling at my body. What do I do?"

> The name of Jesus causes demons to flee, and the blood of the Lamb protects us.

If you are experiencing something like this, do not succumb to these evil spirits but know that God's strength is made perfect in your weakness. (See 2 Corinthians 12:9.) It's time for us to hear how much grace God has for us. It's time to know that only the name of Jesus causes demons to flee and that the blood of the Lamb protects us. Just as the Lord was a wall of fire surrounding Jerusalem, He will also surround you with His glory and power, so that no weapon the enemy forms against you will prosper. (See Zechariah 2:4–5; Isaiah 54:17.)

Remember the following truths during difficult times in order to keep from succumbing to the deceptive voices of seducing spirits.

Know That God Is with You

Even when you feel as if you are alone, God is always there.

> *For He Himself has said, "I will never leave you nor forsake you."* (Hebrews 13:5)

> *If I take the wings of the morning, and dwell in the uttermost parts of the sea, even there Your hand shall lead me, and Your right hand shall hold me. If I say, "Surely the darkness shall fall on me," even the night shall be light about me; indeed, the darkness shall not hide from You, but the night shines as the day.* (Psalm 139:9–12)

Know That God Loves You

The love of God is unconditional. He loves you in spite of the challenges you are currently facing, and He is waiting and willing to receive you to Himself when you call upon His name.

Yes, I have loved you with an everlasting love; therefore with lovingkindness I have drawn you.   (Jeremiah 31:3)

For God so loved the world that He gave His only begotten Son, that whoever believes in Him should not perish but have everlasting life.   (John 3:16)

But God demonstrates His own love toward us, in that while we were still sinners, Christ died for us.   (Romans 5:8)

Who shall separate us from the love of Christ? Shall tribulation, or distress, or persecution, or famine, or nakedness, or peril, or sword? As it is written: "For Your sake we are killed all day long; We are accounted as sheep for the slaughter." Yet in all these things we are more than conquerors through Him who loved us. For I am persuaded that neither death nor life, nor angels nor principalities nor powers, nor things present nor things to come, nor height nor depth, nor any other created thing, shall be able to separate us from the love of God which is in Christ Jesus our Lord.   (Romans 8:35–39)

Call upon Me in the day of trouble; I will deliver you, and you shall glorify Me.
     (Psalm 50:15)

Recognize That God's Word Is True

It is impossible for God to lie. If He made you a promise, He will fulfill it.

God is not a man, that He should lie, nor a son of man, that He should repent. Has He said, and will He not do? Or has He spoken, and will He not make it good?
(Numbers 23:19)

The entirety of Your word is truth, and every one of Your righteous judgments endures forever. (Psalm 119:160)

Your word is truth. (John 17:17)

You do not have to be intimidated by the taunting of satanic threats against you. When you learn the truth in God's Word, you will become less susceptible to the devil's vicious assaults against you. Read and memorize God's promises of protection and deliverance and apply them to your life. Whenever I encounter those who are fearful of the enemy's attacks, I instruct them, "Just tell the devil that you are already dead in Christ Jesus and that you continue to die daily to the things of the world in order to worship and serve the living God." (See Romans 6:4; Galatians 2:20.)

You have to study the Word of God to show yourself approved to God and to remind the devil of who you are in Christ Jesus. (See 2 Timothy 2:15 KJV.) Even in death, victory belongs to those who know their God and are called according to His divine purpose. (See Romans 8:28.)

Don't Give Up!

God said that troubled times would come in the last days (see, for example, Matthew 24:6–7; 2 Timothy 3:1–5), and it breaks my heart when we tell God we are going to serve Him yet give up and return to our old ways because of apathy, guilt, or fear. Our troubled times should not prevent us from serving God and waging warfare against the enemy. If you are struggling, don't quit! Repent and come back to God, and He will help you.

When we call on Jesus in times of trouble, He dispatches very powerful angels on our behalf to deliver us from the hand of the enemy. Sometimes they stand around us, watching over us. They also go into warfare and fight battles for us. They put chains around demons and drag them away. They send fire from their swords, after which God's Word is written in the air. These angels are truly powerful, and God has sent them to minister to us as heirs of salvation.

"Are [angels] *not all ministering spirits sent forth to minister for those who will inherit salvation?"* (Hebrews 1:14).

In visions, I have seen chariots charge out of heaven, guided by angels who continually come to our rescue when we earnestly seek God in prayer. These war angels are very fierce-looking and are focused on their purpose of fulfilling the will of God. They have jaws of iron and eyes of fire. Their garments are made out of metal and iron, as well as other material I could not identify. They wear helmets, are adorned with the gar-ments of warfare, and fight fiercely with demons on our

> The more we believe God, the more the heavenly hosts fight on our behalf.

behalf. These angels of the Lord go all over the earth. With their huge swords of fire, they cut the evil presence and powers of darkness.

The more we believe God, the more the heav-enly hosts fight against the devil on our behalf. The more we study and apply the Word of God, the more they deliver. Be encouraged, because *"joy comes in the morning"* (Psalm 30:5).

What I have learned and am still learning about angels is how real and powerful they are, and how God sometimes allows us to see them.

Many years ago, my child had a very high fever, and I had been praying for days for his fever to break. I had his bed by mine, and as I was praying one day, strange things began to happen. A bright light appeared in the bedroom. In this circle of light was the face of an angel with the most beautiful hair. The only way I can describe its color is to compare it to a bright carrot. He also held a sword. I looked at my son and God opened my eyes to see the spirit of fever on him. It was wrapped around him like a caterpillar and it was black. Yet there was a prominent look of determination upon the angel's face. He pointed the sword at my son's body, and when he did, he commanded the spirit of fever to come off. It fled and wrapped around the sword of the angel. The angel then lifted the sword and exited with it through the window. Immediately, my son was delivered from the fever.

I have seen angels work to bring God's Word to pass, and believe me, His Word cannot fail. God wants you to know that you hold the power to change your circumstances through the name of Jesus and by invoking His power upon every circumstance that threatens to bring about your demise.

Fight the good fight of faith, lay hold on eternal life, to which you were also called

*and have confessed the good confession in
the presence of many witnesses.*
(1 Timothy 6:12)

You will never receive the benefits of the warfare going on in the heavenly realm by constantly
giving up on the things of God. You have to fight
and remain faithful to God in order to lay hold of
eternal life because the enemy will do everything
possible to keep you from obtaining it. It is a fight
of faith, but remember that God has already won
it on your behalf. Wherever you go, and regardless of what you go through in life, continue seeking the Lord, and He will reveal an answer to
your needs.

8

DELIVERANCE THROUGH PRAYER

I now want to discuss intercessory prayer, which is a powerful weapon in deliverance. Paul admonished us, *"Praying always with all prayer and supplication in the Spirit, being watchful to this end with all perseverance and supplication for all the saints"* (Ephesians 6:18).

When God allows me to see supernatural manifestations, I sometimes see demons on the shoulders or legs of people, or whispering in their ears. The demons do not always possess the people, but they *oppress* them. Because many people have not been taught how to pray and reject demonic influences, they don't always know how to fight against them. In this chapter, I want to help you understand how to pray for yourself and others to be set free.

WALK IN YOUR CALLING

One of the gifts God has given me is the gift of mercy and love. After I saw the visions of hell, I was never the same again. Beforehand, I did not understand the driving force behind the depth of horrible sins people commit. Now, when I pray for someone, I can earnestly travail for him to be set free by the power of God because I possess the revelation that's necessary to connect with his need to be delivered. I have the calling of God upon me to act on what He has anointed me to do. I earnestly admonish others to do the same—to walk in the calling of God upon their lives.

> Who stood in the gap for you? You need to intercede for others in the same way.

Thousands in our land are dying as a result of people's bondages and sin. I know that God wants a change in the earth. We must let the Father know we love Him by the way we love others. When you were in need—spiritually lost, struggling with addiction, sick, or helpless—who prayed for you? Who stood in the gap for you? Who wanted you to overcome? The Spirit of the Lord was persuading people to intercede on your behalf. You need to intercede for others in the same way.

When you have been called by God, you can't follow the crowd. God does not want copycats. He wants you to be led and taught by His Spirit. Some people would rather turn a deaf ear to the Word of the Lord, close their eyes to His spiritual foresight, and harden their hearts because to receive truth and take responsibility also means we have to *change* and do things God's way. Change can be very inconvenient to our lifestyle and ways of doing things; nonetheless, God commands it. We must repent of our selfishness and return to the foot of the cross.

Perhaps you don't feel worthy or able to intercede for others. Again, though you may sometimes stumble and fall in your journey of faith, this does not mean you should turn from God and give up. You might get bumps and bruises on your way down, but if you reach up to Him, the Lord will alleviate the pain with His healing balm from heaven. Regardless of what you are going through, God has an answer to relieve every affliction; He has all knowledge and can provide you with a peaceful solution. Reach out to God, and He will make you an overcomer, able to rise above everything that is trying to take you under. Then you can minister to others in turn.

We must believe God and let go of our doubt and fear. We have to believe that God is a dwelling place, and that if we do sin, we can still go to Him in repentance and receive forgiveness through Christ. (See 1 John 1:7–9.) If He has to prune us again, so be it. The Lord chastens us because of His undying love for us and His commitment to saving our souls and the souls of others. Therefore, repent, have communion with God, and allow Him to cleanse your heart. Seek Him in earnest prayer, such as this one:

> Lord, I believe I have victory through Christ over every area of my life. I repent of my sins. [Name them.] I ask You to cover my entire household with Your blood and Your Word so that no weapons formed against it shall prosper. Hold me close to You; teach me and guide me today. In Jesus' name, amen.

This type of prayer, along with the Lord's Prayer, is what I ask people to pray when they seek me for advice concerning spiritual attacks. Pray these prayers every day so that they will become a part of your daily walk with God.

The Power of Prayer

When you pray, remember that Jesus has all power and authority. (See Matthew 28:18.) We must put these demonic influences under His feet, in His name. (See Psalm 8:6; 110:1; 1 Corinthians 15:25–27.) I have seen visions of people praying, and their prayers go up like beams of light. As they approach the throne, the prayers appear as written words, and God commands them to return to the earth in the form of an answer.

As we are in this prayerful state, the enemy will be held back. It becomes impossible for him to penetrate the protection of prayer. Demons flee and report to the devil, "We could not attack them because of this hedge of prayer." I have seen visions of this actually happening. I have seen people pray and have witnessed a circular hedge of fire coming up to protect entire families.

> **As we are in this prayerful state, the enemy will be held back.**

Let me give you another example of the power of prayer. There was a little boy whom I used to minister to and encourage in the Lord. I told him, "Honey, if you ever get into trouble, call upon the name of Jesus Christ." Little did I know that just two weeks later, this little boy would be in a car accident. He was a passenger in the backseat, and the car tumbled over an embankment and landed in the river. The car sank, and it took about fifteen minutes to get him and the other passengers out of the car. Unfortunately, two of the young men died, but this young boy miraculously survived. In the hospital, after the medics had pumped his stomach, he told the medical staff, "I remembered what Mrs. Baxter said—to call upon the name of Jesus. And when we were in that car, I kept praying, 'Jesus, save me!' and it's like an air bubble formed around my head and I could breathe. I remember breathing until they pulled me out, and I know it was because of the name of Jesus." I hear many stories about the power of prayer in Jesus' name.

Prayer against the Gates of Hell

Years ago, I had a vision of one of the gates of hell while I was on a preaching trip in Pennsylvania. There was a place in the woods there where satanic worshippers practiced rituals with symbols on the ground and all kinds of demonic activity. A group of us, all of whom were Christians, went there to anoint the ground because one man was terrified by the demonic activity that was taking place in this area. We had anointing oil, and we opened the Bible and asked God to send His army of angels to shut this gate of hell. As we prayed, the earth shook and the ground began to sink. Then I saw the angels of God come and put a chain and a lock upon the door that led to that gate of hell.

We experienced a demonic attack after we performed this prayer, so that the car we were riding in got stuck on a broken sewer line. It was very cold at the time and, as the sewer line broke, sewage spilled all over the car. I kept reminding the people that it was only the response of the enemy, who was trying to harass us after we had fulfilled the will of the Lord.

After you do the work of the Lord, the enemy tries to bombard you with aggravation to make you question whether or not you were in the will of God. But the Bible assures us that whatever we bind on earth will be bound in heaven, and whatever is loosed on earth will be loosed in heaven.

> I believe the living Word of God, which I have stood on against satanic attack.

None of us was injured in this incident, and after we freed the car from the broken sewer line, we were able to see that it was just another satanic distraction that was attempting to take away from the miracle that had occurred after our intercession. I believe the living Word of God. We stood on the Word of God and rejoiced at the fact that the gates of hell could not use even this foul situation to prevail against us. "The gates of hell shall not prevail" is not a cliché; it is the living Word of

God, which I have witnessed on a number of occasions throughout my ministerial travels.

Another time, when I was preaching in a different state, I received a call from a lady who asked, "Since you're preaching about the gates of hell, can you please come to my house and anoint my yard and pray with me because my husband has lost his mind?"

"How did he lose his mind?" I asked.

"He believes that there are aliens that transport him out of the home and into this spaceship to do awful things to him."

"Really?" I responded curiously. So I asked some people to go with me to pray for this lady. As I entered her house, I smelled a foul odor and immediately turned to her and asked, "What in the world is that?"

She responded, "Come on; I'll show you." She opened a screen door at the back of the house, and there in her backyard were at least two inches of dog dung spread out in a big circle.

"Every dog in this subdivision comes to my house to relieve himself in my backyard," she explained.

I told her to give me a bottle of olive oil, and I immediately began to pray. I walked around the edge of this huge circle of dog dung and began to call upon the Lord to shut this gate of hell and stop the attack of the enemy on her family. As I prayed, the ground sank about eight inches. Suddenly, I saw a vision of angels coming and sealing that gate. They bound it with a chain, locked it up, and began singing the victory. "Dear God," I said, "these gates are truly real!" I began to fully understand all the times that God had anointed me to pray over the land while visiting other cities, where I would see the fire of God come down and destroy the evil forces of Satan. So I began to pay close attention to cities and towns throughout my travels. I had visions of God reaching His arm down and burning up the darkness, and I was so happy. I prayed, "God, we need a revival. We need to revive the people, and they need to get their minds clear of the devil's mentality and be renewed by the mind of Christ."

PRAYER FOR DELIVERANCE FROM BONDAGE

Recently, some intercessors and I went into deep prayer and travail that the spirit of drug addiction would be bound in the name of Jesus in the life of a certain person. We prayed for him continually. We had known this dear individual for quite a while and his tragic situation just broke our hearts. This was a very precious person who had had a reputation for working hard and making a good salary. Yet, one day, I heard that he was on drugs and living on the streets. This touched my heart so deeply that I would travail and cry for him because he appeared to have no more control over his life. He had lost all self-respect. At one point, we almost gave up praying for him, but we could not. I knew I had to continue in travail—not only for him, but also for many others in the earth who were battling this same demonic force.

My heart was seriously broken because of the massive drug use and the number of children who were dying or getting arrested and going to jail. So many people need to know that there is a way of escape, that God Almighty can deliver them from the demon of drugs. I know many parents who have had family members on drugs, and it is very heartbreaking. It hurts people so deeply that we need a mass healing from the deep wounds of drug abuse.

> So many people need to know there is a way of escape. God can deliver them.

One evening, at six o'clock, I was greatly travailing in the Spirit for this man and others on drugs. As I was praying, a heaviness suddenly seemed to drop on me, accompanied by grief for these young people. The Spirit of God came upon me, and I just shut my eyes and continued to travail. Later, I remember going to get a drink of water, and as I looked at the clock I noticed that it was midnight, but I still did not have a release regarding this burden for souls to be saved. When the Lord has placed a burden upon you to stand in the gap and pray for certain things, He gives you the gift of the power of the Holy Spirit to see into the spirit realm and to pray until there is a release.

I kept praying, and as I went to refresh myself again, I noticed that the time was now three in the morning, but the Spirit was still upon me to continue praying. I began to quote the Word of the Lord and rely on God's promises for added strength, such as, *"Call upon Me in the day of trouble; I will deliver you, and you shall glorify Me"* (Psalm 50:15). There is deliverance in the name of Jesus Christ. In faith, I applied to the situation whatever Scripture came to me by the Holy Spirit, and I decreed the victory by the power of God. (See Job 22:28.)

By six in the morning, I could see the sun peeking through the hills. My body was tired, but I felt the joy of the Lord. I prayed by the power of Christ Jesus that God would answer this prayer. All at once, I had a mighty vision. Heaven opened up, and two or three angels were standing outside the heavenly gates. They had sheets of paper on which were listed the names of people from the earth. The angel of the Lord let me understand that these were the people for whom the intercessors and I had been praying, who were suffering from drugs and all kinds of other addictions.

I saw the gates of heaven swing open, and out of them came droves of war angels riding on horses or chariots. The angels were about thirty feet tall, and they had jaws of iron and eyes of fire. Their entire bodies were adorned with beautiful armor made out of brass, copper, and gold. On their sides were swords as large as men. The swords glowed with flames that shot from both ends. These warring angels were given orders to come to the earth and deliver the people.

When I saw the beauty of this army, I began shouting and praising God. The way they looked, they could penetrate any darkness. I knew that the world needed to know about God's army— the army that is called to deliver us in the day of trouble.

I put my trust in the Lord, and then I had a vision of different parts of the earth; I could peer into the ghettos, parks, and houses. I saw all this in color; it was as if the scenes of a television program were unfolding right before my very eyes.

Scenes of people's plights began to flash sporadically before me: some of the people were in alleys, being beaten up; some were drunk and falling down on the ground; others were in their homes suffering in turmoil. I saw one boy near a dumpster in an alley, and someone was beating him to death with a club. He was shirtless as he lay on the ground, unconscious. I didn't want him to die, and I realized that the man who was beating him was demonically possessed.

When witnessing a situation this devastating, you might think to yourself, *How do I even begin to pray?* You pray for the will of God and for the Holy Spirit to speak through you to say the right words. Then you yield yourself to God and allow His Spirit to pray through you as you trust and believe Him. He's the King of kings and Lord of lords, and when He speaks a word, He exercises diligence to perform it.

> When you pray, ask the Holy Spirit to speak through you to say the right words.

As this image faded away, I saw an influx of angels suddenly arrive on earth. They went into the towns and cities, into the streets, parks, and people's homes. I could see people who had black forms wrapped around them that looked like monkeys. The angels would rip the hands off these demonic creatures and cremate them. As the angels wrenched these figures from people, the people would shake and tremble while their deliverance was taking place. The angels would touch them and they would drop to their knees, praying and crying under the anointing of God.

Other demonic images appeared in the form of rats or snakes. I could see an angel move its hands down an alley, and the demons would be cremated and turned to ashes. At the sight of this, I began to rejoice because God was showing me His deliverance power. He was reminding me that if we call upon the Lord, stand in the gap, and pray for people to be free of their sins, He will send help from His sanctuary.

The Lord continued to show me instances of His power in action. For example, a man was sitting on a barstool and drinking. Angels pulled one demon from his shoulder, another demon from his side, and a third demon from his mouth. The man began shaking his head in disbelief. He asked, "What's happening to me? What's happening to me?" When he stepped outside the bar, the power of God hit him. He began to cry and fell to his knees to be saved. Demonic powers had been preventing him from giving himself completely to Jesus Christ, but now he was set free.

The Lord revealed to me, "You're seeing My deliverance power through prayer." I continued to watch as people whom the angels were delivering went into the streets. I would see dark shadows upon the people and shadowy figures on their legs. As the angels wrenched these figures off the people, the people would shake and tremble while their deliverance was taking place.

This vision went on for hours and hours, and the Lord said, "There will be a mighty deliverance in the earth. You watch and you see." It was wonderful to see the Lord setting the captives free. The Lord impressed on me to write the vision down and to talk about it. He wanted me to emphasize the fact that He is our Deliverer and we are never to give up hope in prayer, in asking Jesus to intervene.

When I saw the Word of God in action, I began to comprehend the extreme necessity of praying and commanding evil spirits to loose those who are bound. We need to understand that God can change the heart and save the soul of anyone. He cares about us that much.

In the next few months of my ministry, as I traveled and preached about hell and what God had shown me, young men and women would come up to me at the book table or at the altar of the church where I was ministering, and they would share with me their testimonies, which were similar to this:

> Just a few weeks ago we were delivered and healed by the power of God. I came out of this bar so drunk, and I sobered up, dropped to my knees, and accepted the Lord.

Over and over, testimonies were being reported. I want the world to know that there is hope in Jesus Christ. He is our Healer and Deliverer. He showed me visions of His Word setting the captives free as God's people stand in the gap and make a hedge of protection around those for whom they are praying. We have to keep praying and believing God Almighty for deliverance in Jesus' name.

> *The LORD is my rock and my fortress and my deliverer; my God, my strength, in whom I will trust; my shield and the horn of my salvation, my stronghold.*
>
> (Psalm 18:2)

PRAYER AGAINST INVISIBLE FORCES OF EVIL

I feel blessed to be able to see many manifestations of the spirit realm, yet this only happens when the Lord allows it. One time, I was grieved over people's sins because they seemed to have no reverence for God, and they were mocking Him. During this time, I had been seeking God for answers concerning certain matters. While I was coming out of my hotel one evening at twilight, I began to look at the people walking. I didn't have to preach that particular night, and the Lord said to me, "Look." He opened my eyes to see a demon walking two feet from someone and talking to him. He showed me another person on a bicycle who had a demon sitting on his shoulder. I would see people with demons wrapped around their legs and the individuals would be limping. Demons would be wrapped around the arms of others and their arms would be bandaged.

The Lord informed me that the enemy had done this. He had caused afflictions, heartaches, and grief. Then the Spirit of the Lord instructed me, saying, "Child, pray for these people." I went back to my room and I prayed for them. For several days, during the twilight hours, I would actually see these spirits in airports. Off and on, throughout the year, I would see these things again, and I would continue to pray. The people were not aware that evil spirits were causing their afflictions. They could not see them, and I would not have been able to see them, either, except that God allowed me to observe them in the Spirit.

In a church service where I was ministering, the Lord revealed someone to me and I called this individual up to pray for him. As I interceded on his behalf, God allowed me to witness his complete deliverance right before my eyes as he was loosed from the bondage that had ruled his life. For years, this young man had been bound by demonic strongholds, but in an instant, the Spirit of the Lord set him free.

God has given me the spirit of healing in praying for people. I have witnessed miraculous testimonies everywhere, especially in other countries. I have even seen God create brand new brain cells.

One time, I prayed for a little girl who was so sick she could not hold her head up. The Lord showed me a serpent wrapped around her neck and instructed me to pray in the Holy Spirit. As I prayed, I saw angels yank that demonic spirit from her. I then asked God to restore the muscles in her little neck so she could hold her head up again.

At other times, I have seen an evil spirit upon someone's intestines, and when I cast it out, the individual was healed. Or I have seen a dark spot on a person's lung. This was a spirit of infirmity that had attached itself, and I cast it out in Jesus' name. Only through the name of Jesus and His mercy does He reveal these things to me in order to help humanity.

Many people unknowingly suffer from sicknesses and diseases that come from the gates of hell to steal, kill, and destroy. (See John 10:10.) This is why the power of loosing and binding must be taught and acted upon with power and authority in the name of Jesus.

One of the most memorable visions I have had involved the healing of a ten-year-old boy many years ago. This boy was my son's best friend at the time. He was a diabetic, and I would sometimes take care of him. At one point, he became gravely ill and fell into a diabetic coma. As I sat in the hospital room by the bedside of this child, I continuously prayed, and I fasted. All at once, God opened my eyes to see that on the top of his head was the outline of what appeared to be a transparent scorpion. His tentacles were sticking in this child, and he had the boy's head in his mouth as he lay there. As I continued to pray and rebuke the devil, the Spirit of the Lord spoke to me and said, "I'm going to teach you how to pray against this situation. This is a diabetes demon. This is a

> The power of loosing and binding in the name of Jesus must be taught and acted upon.

scorpion demon spirit that is sent into the earth to destroy the people. I've given you authority over the power of this scorpion."

As I watched, I became aware of the cruelty of this demonic force. I did not know anything about this evil spirit, but I began to pray by the life, the power, and the blood of Jesus Christ. I asked God, in Jesus' name, to loosen those tentacles from that child and for that demon to let him go. As I did this, the room filled with angels. They had a scroll and the Word of God, and they began to loosen the tentacles. I watched this great deliverance taking place upon the boy, and I began to praise the Lord. As they pulled this thing off him, I saw the angels put a chain around it and drag it out the window and into the sky—far away to "dry places." (See Matthew 12:43; Luke 11:24.)

I looked back at the child, and he shook his head and came out of the coma. The Lord said, "Now pray for restoration—to restore the blood sugar, to restore the blood level, and for the pancreas to be healed." He was instructing me about what to do and how to pray for this child, and I was overjoyed that He had chosen me to pray for him and to see him out of this coma. As the nurses came in, I continued praying silently and thanking God for the miracle that had taken place.

For I am the LORD who heals you.
(Exodus 15:26)

Another vision I had concerning the kingdom of darkness happened many years ago. During a time when I had been in much prayer, the Lord took me and showed me the galaxies. He showed me the prince of the power of the air and how demons hinder answers to our prayers, as we read about in the book of Daniel. (See Daniel 10:1–14.) He began to reveal to me the necessity of our having a strategic plan to incorporate prayer into our lives. If we do not know how to pray, we should ask God to teach us. Jesus has blessed us to have dominion in His name, and we begin to see the manifestation of this dominion as we seek Him earnestly in prayer.

> **If we do not know how to pray, we should ask God to teach us.**

In one of my visions of angels fighting demonic powers, it seemed as if some of the angels were overcome and had somehow become bound by chains themselves. I began to watch this and pray, and for months I became engrossed in deep travail. While praying, I saw a vision of these angels flash before my eyes. Some were trying to fight for us and protect us. They were being attacked by the biggest demon I had ever seen, and warfare was being waged fiercely between the demonic spirits and the angels of God. I began to quote the Word of the Lord as the Holy Spirit led me.

Months later, I was in deep travail, and a pastor and I were sharing the Word of God when all at once this vision became very strong and vivid. It appeared as a large honeycomb with several compartments. It hovered high above the earth, and demons were sealing something inside each of the compartments. Puzzled, I thought, *God, what is this?* as I continued praying and quoting the Word of the Lord, beckoning God for deliverance. I then saw angels go in and break open those sealed compartments and rescue the angels who had been held up by these demonic forces. The Lord delivered these angels who had been in warfare with the devil as another group of angels came who were mightier and stronger than the first group to destroy these demonic powers by the thousands. We must realize that we are fighting against powerful forces, but we have the victory in the name of Jesus as we persevere in prayer.

THE SECRET TO ANSWERED PRAYER

God has allowed me to witness many beautiful things through the Holy Spirit. Many years before I had begun sharing my visions of hell and angels, the Lord appeared to me and I went with Him. He showed me various cities and towns, and as He would drop balls of fire over them, revival would begin to take place in each one.

Once, I was in a certain city, and I had been praying for the move of the Holy Spirit to go through that place. In a vision, I saw the city streets and the mountainous terrains. Down the mountainside came the white glory of God flowing like a river—a living river drifting over the trees and hills. It then flowed into certain homes, and in each of those homes a great revival would break out.

> God wants us to pray so salvation and healing can take place around the world.

People would be asleep in their beds, and the angels would go and shake them awake; these people would jump up and start to pray. I would see other people, however, who remained asleep when the angels tried to awaken them. The angels would then knock on their doors, but no one would answer. Nevertheless, I saw a great revival come to the city, and I praised the Lord.

God wants us to pray so that salvation, revival, deliverance, and healing can take place across the nation and around the world. The secret to witnessing the miraculous is really not a big secret at all. It simply requires faith in God to do what you have asked of Him in your time of need.

The Scriptures tell us that after Jesus had traveled from Bethany to Jerusalem, He was very hungry. Seeing a fig tree in the distance, He went to it, but He found no fruit on its branches. Jesus immediately cursed the fig tree: *"Let no one eat fruit from you ever again"* (Mark 11:14).

The following morning, as Jesus and His disciples passed the fig tree, Peter was amazed when he noticed that the fig tree had dried up, and he brought this fact to Jesus' attention: *"Rabbi, look! The fig tree which You cursed has withered away"* (v. 21). Peter was surprised, but Jesus was not shocked at all. He knew His word was truth and that it was incapable of failing to do what He had commanded. Jesus simply replied to Peter, *"Have faith in God"* (v. 22). He then went on to remind Peter that all believers hold this same power. (See verses 23–24.)

When we earnestly believe in God, our faith can move mountains. Whether you are praying for yourself or for others, you cannot allow anything to damage your faith in God, for if you do, you will hinder your prayers and delay the deliverance.

Jesus answered and said to them, "Assuredly, I say to you, if you have faith and do not doubt, you will not only do what was done to the fig tree, but also if you say to this mountain, 'Be removed and be cast into the sea,' it will be done. And whatever things you ask in prayer, believing, you will receive." (Matthew 21:21–22)

WHY PRAYERS MAY NOT BE ANSWERED

Besides a lack of faith, there are other reasons for unanswered prayer, including the following.

The Wrong Timing

Regardless of how much you believe, if it is not in God's timing, you will not see the manifestation of your request. You will need to wait until God decrees it is time to bring the answer to fruition. It is during such a time of waiting, however, that many people become frustrated and give up, even though they are right at the brink of realizing their miracles. God does not always reveal the answer immediately, but this does not mean He hasn't answered the prayer.

When Jesus cursed the fig tree, it wasn't until the next morning that Peter noticed it had withered away; however, the tree was as good as withered the moment Jesus spoke the word. Again, even though you do not yet see the answer to your prayers, this does not mean that God's promise has not been fulfilled. Continue to believe, regardless of what you see in the natural, and you will soon witness the physical manifestation of your request. *"Faith is the substance of things hoped for, the evidence of things not seen"* (Hebrews 11:1).

Unforgiveness against Others

Throughout the Word of God, the Lord warns us of the hindrances that we bring upon ourselves when we hold grudges against others and do not forgive.

> *Whatever things you ask when you pray, believe that you receive them, and you will have them. And whenever you stand praying, if you have anything against anyone, forgive him, that your Father in heaven may also forgive you your trespasses.*
>
> (Mark 11:24–25)

Before we can see the full manifestation of God's glory and power, we must *"lay aside every weight, and the sin which so easily ensnares us"* (Hebrews 12:1)—including bitterness and unforgiveness.

Half-hearted Prayer

If we do not pray at all, or if we pray in a half-hearted way, we cannot expect to receive.

The effective, fervent prayer of a righteous man avails much.   (James 5:16)

Rejoicing in hope, patient in tribulation, continuing steadfastly in prayer.
(Romans 12:12)

HOW TO PRAY

Many people want to know how they should pray. It isn't necessarily the length of the prayer that counts. Jesus said, *"And when you pray, do not use vain repetitions as the heathen do. For they think that they will be heard for their many words"* (Matthew 6:7). Rather, it is the quality of the prayer that gets God's attention. Jesus told us how to enter God's presence through five essential elements in His model prayer, which has come to be called the Lord's Prayer.

1. **Worship**: *"Our Father in heaven, hallowed be Your name"* (v. 9).
2. **Praying the will of the Father**: *"Your kingdom come. Your will be done on earth as it is in heaven"* (v. 10).
3. **Asking the Father to meet your need**: *"Give us this day our daily bread"* (v. 11).
4. **Repentance/Forgiveness**: *"And forgive us our debts, as we forgive our debtors"* (v. 12).

5. **Holiness**: *"And do not lead us into temptation, but deliver us from the evil one. For Yours is the kingdom and the power and the glory forever. Amen"* (v. 13).

It is equally important to keep these vital components in mind when conducting spiritual warfare. Spiritual warfare is taking authority over whatever is keeping you or the subject of your intercession bound. It's not excellency of speech or physical antics that invoke the anointing and power of God, but rather your ability to summon God's presence through the vigilance of effective prayer.

> To be prepared for battle, you must be in a right relationship with God.

The anointing of God destroys every yoke. (See Isaiah 10:27.) God warns that we are not to enter into spiritual warfare haphazardly; we are to be properly prepared for battle. *"Do not lay hands on anyone hastily, nor share in other people's sins; keep yourself pure"* (1 Timothy 5:22). *"Put on the whole armor of God, that you may be able to stand against the wiles of the devil"* (Ephesians 6:11). Those who are prepared for battle are in right relationship with God. They are wearing their spiritual armor and have the Holy Spirit's anointing. These are the ones who are effective in exposing Satan's deception, closing gateways to hell, and setting captives free.

THE ROLE OF FASTING IN SPIRITUAL WARFARE

Finally, we must realize that we may need to fast as well as pray when conducting spiritual warfare for deliverance. Once, when Jesus' disciples asked Him why they could not cast out a certain demon, He answered, *"This kind does not go out except by prayer and fasting"* (Matthew 17:21).

In addition to praying and studying the Word of God, fasting is a vital part of the Christian experience. During a fast, the spirit of man avails itself to hear from the Lord in a special way through the denial of food. Denying the flesh through fasting can help us to maintain the purity and power of our relationship with God. Often, we hear more from God and learn more about Him and His ways through fasting than we ever could otherwise.

Jesus taught us the proper way to fast:

Moreover, when you fast, do not be like the hypocrites, with a sad countenance. For they disfigure their faces that they may appear to men to be fasting. Assuredly, I say to you, they have their reward. But you, when you fast, anoint your head and wash your face, so that you do not appear to men

> *to be fasting, but to your Father who is in*
> *the secret place; and your Father who sees*
> *in secret will reward you openly.*
>
> (Matthew 6:16–18)

Without a doubt, although our physical bodies can seem weak when we are fasting, our spirits are being strengthened and drawn closer to God. Fasting intensifies the believer's faith and better equips him with the power to combat spiritual wickedness in heavenly places. Although the Lord Jesus Christ already defeated the devil on our behalf, fasting can give us the spiritual rejuvenation that we need to walk in the victory the Lord has made available to us.

Fasting not only opens our spirits to hear from God, but it is also an act of worship. Giving up food to draw closer to the Lord is an intimate sacrifice that we give to Him and which He graciously accepts.

When we fast, however, we must also be prepared for challenges. We may experience the resistance of the flesh and the enemy. Sometimes, it can seem that the more we seek God, the more the attacks begin to mount against us. For example, it can be an inner battle to maintain the sacrifice while simultaneously listening for the voice of God. Have you ever noticed, for instance, that when you go on a fast, even if you are normally a light eater, all you can think about is food? You may also experience other distractions or disruptions. We must be aware of these challenges and prepare for them.

The purpose of fasting is not to show others how spiritual we are. It is a true sacrifice only when our motives are in the right place. Yet as we sacrifice to God in secret, Jesus said the Father will reward us openly.

STANDING IN THE GAP

I really believe in the power of prayer through the Holy Spirit and in the name of Jesus. We do not always know how to pray. Yet if we earnestly seek the Lord and pray to Him in the Spirit, then the Spirit will make intercession for us according to His will, and His will for our lives cannot fail.

Likewise the Spirit also helps in our weaknesses. For we do not know what we should pray for as we ought, but the Spirit Himself makes intercession for us with groanings which cannot be uttered. Now He who searches the hearts knows what the mind of the Spirit is, because He makes intercession for the saints according to the will of God. (Romans 8:26–27)

We can pray and fast for the deliverance of our loved ones and friends. In His righteousness, God desires to save whole households. That is His promise, and He has kept His promise to me in this regard: *"Believe on the Lord Jesus Christ, and you will be saved, you and your household"* (Acts 16:31).

When your heart is pure before the Lord, and when you call upon His name as you stand in the gap for others, He will destroy the demonic powers that are attacking them. You can take dominion over demonic forces and command them to flee. You can take authority over the "strong man" (see, for example, Matthew 12:29), pulling him down and putting him under your feet in Jesus' name.

> *And whatever things you ask in prayer, believing, you will receive.* (Matthew 21:22)

9

DELIVERANCE THROUGH THE WORD

Even though we live in troubled times and many people are being oppressed by the enemy, I have decided this: regardless of what the present and future generations hold, I am going to preach the truth concerning God's Word so strongly it will demand an audience—both with those who are searching for truth and those who are still living in rebellion—so all can know how to escape the devices of Satan.

The Word of God has the power to set people free:

> *For the word of God is living and powerful, and sharper than any two-edged sword, piercing even to the division of soul and spirit, and of joints and marrow, and is a discerner of the thoughts and intents of the heart.* (Hebrews 4:12)

The Truth of the Word Sets You Free

The more you pay attention to God's truth in the Scriptures and receive it as an applicable component of your life, the more evil spirits must flee and make way for the blessings of God to come upon your life. I have seen God's angels destroying demonic spirits as they attempted to come against the children of God. God watches over you as you plead the blood of Jesus and claim the name of Jesus over your life.

Hide the Word of God in your heart, and the peace of God that surpasses all human understanding will overtake you. Regardless of what demonic weapons form against you, when you know how to rebuke the devil in the name of Jesus, these weapons will not prosper. Let me give you an illustration of this.

> Hide the Word of God in your heart, and the peace of God will overtake you.

A young man had been troubled since he was a little boy by a demon coming to his bedroom. In his first year of college, he encountered a group of people talking about orbs, which are translucent balls of light that tend to appear in "haunted" places. This group told him that "nice" spirits appear to people at night to give them orbs, and that in 2012 there would be a shift in the spirit realm that would take place on their behalf. I found out that this form of doctrine is being presented all over the world. This is a demonic agenda fueled by demonic powers.

Another gentleman, who is a Christian, prayed for this young college student to be set free from the influences of these demonic strongholds. After he prayed for the student, the demon that had visited this young man since his childhood manifested itself again. It went to his room to give him an orb. Yet when the orb came into his room, this time, he rebuked it according to God's Word in order to be set free. Once he knew the truth and received it, the Word of God immediately delivered him.

And you shall know the truth, and the truth shall make you free.   (John 8:32)

Many of our young people are wrapped up in satanic rituals and doctrines. They think it's fine to dabble in demonic spirits as a fad to fit in with their peers. Yet this is a deception from the gates of hell. Whether you call yourself a white witch or a black witch, it is an abomination to God because witches and warlocks seek to summon up demons and all types of wickedness to go forth and invoke the manifestation of their will upon others.

These are the things that God Almighty is exposing today because He wants you to know His Word will help you in every situation—even to break free from satanic involvement and the debilitating strongholds that have limited you for years.

REVEALING THE TRUTH

When God calls someone as a prophet of the Lord, he or she must go through various times of testing. It might be a test of obedience, or a test that will ultimately reveal the truth and power of God's Word. In every situation, the person must believe God's Word, regardless of what is happening around him or her.

After God called me and placed me in the ministry, it was quite a while before He revealed to me the unmistakable reality of hell. But after that time, I would periodically see a vision of a dragon. Every year, for sixteen years, during a period of deep prayer and travail to God, this image would appear, and I knew that there was much warfare taking place.

An account of a great fight involving a dragon with seven heads is recorded in the book of Revelation. It describes how the angels of God fought against the dragon, which was lying in wait to devour the child whom the woman was about to give birth to. The Scriptures describe the victory over this great dragon, revealing the protection of God, His many blessings, and how Jesus watches over the innocent. (See Revelation 12:1–11.)

In my visions of the dragon, the beast had fangs like a serpent, but its tail was that of a dragon. Its seven heads were connected to long necks that extended high into the galaxies. I have come to believe the dragon with seven heads represents the false teachings against our Lord and Savior and the warfare that we experience in trying to release the Word of the Lord to His people.

While in deep travail against false religions and false teachings that contradicted the Word of God, I would encounter part of this vision, and I began to understand the dragon repre-

> **God's Word can set you free from the strongholds that have held you for years.**

sented seven major kingdoms that come against the Word of the Lord. I would pray in the Holy Spirit, rebuking the power of darkness, and binding and loosing. As I did this, huge angels would come from heaven and bind this beastly image with a mighty chain, and there would be tremendous warfare. Then the vision would suddenly vanish.

When I would see this dragon in the heavenlies, its neck would stretch out to attack something in my ministry. I knew it was the *"prince of the power of the air,"* the rulers of demon darkness, and the spiritual wickedness in high places. (See Ephesians 2:2; 6:12.) I understood, through the revelation of God, that this was the warfare He refers to in the Scriptures, and that we must use the name of Jesus to bind the devil and put these things under our feet.

The Holy Spirit began to teach me how to war against this attack of the enemy. The assaults against my ministry always seemed to manifest weeks prior to my having this vision of the warfare that was taking place in the heavenly realm. There would be hindrances through finances, sicknesses, and other situations. Yet, as we stood and proclaimed the Word of the Lord, I could see God's Word in action. I would actually see His angels coming and fighting for us. I could see an open book, and out of it would come the Word of the Lord, which transformed into a two-edged sword. The angels would fight the demon powers over and over, bind them with chains, and carry them to dark places.

When I sought the Lord's counsel about this vision, shortly afterward I had another vision that again included this seven-headed dragon. I saw the world and a pair of justice scales. One end of the justice scale was attacked by a huge serpent.

It seemed to me that there was an unjust balance on this scale, and I did not know who was holding the arm of the scale. As I watched this vision, the one who held the scale turned into the devil himself.

As I sought the face of the Lord, I understood that the enemy was bringing false balances and deception into our lives because his mission is to spread lies and hypocrisy. The devil is bringing many things into our lives to tip the scales of justice against us, and I knew I had to pray to bind him and bring release.

UNCOVERING DECEPTION

As we saw in chapter one, many people, especially in the younger generation, are being engulfed by the ungodly influences of false religions. These false teachings disguise themselves as self-help, self-awareness, and avenues of experiencing personal fulfillment; yet their final result is widespread deception.

Some false doctrines teach that we do not need God, and that everything we require for self-fulfillment lies within us. Other doctrines rely on physical, man-made images as their source of fulfillment; they teach the worship of idols. Again, anything that consumes your attention more than God is your object of worship. Many people have been conned by the teachings of satanic doctrine, but God is very clear concerning His view of idol worship.

> *For you shall worship no other god, for the
> LORD, whose name is Jealous, is a jealous
> God.* (Exodus 34:14)

We serve a God who will not allow anyone or anything to stand in the way of the worship that rightly belongs to Him. Regardless of how many doctrines we may study that promote other gods, the Lord makes it very clear that we are to worship *"no other god."* To reject this commandment is to turn your back on your Creator and Savior. Living without God brings an imbalance to

We serve a God who will not allow anything to steal the worship that belongs to Him.

people's lives that can only be corrected through repentance and an acceptance of the Lord Jesus Christ as Lord and Savior.

The dragon with the seven heads wrestles against the truth of God's Word, but God is the Victor. As ambassadors of the gospel (see 2 Corinthians 5:20), we must speak God's truth and engage in spiritual warfare by commanding the devil to release people. In order to help people come to

Christ, we have to battle false teachings. These teachings never tell you about being born again; they rarely warn you of your negative behavior or reveal that if you call upon the name of the Lord, He will save you. They hide the fact that no matter what you have done, God's love will reach out to save, heal, and deliver you; that God Almighty is there to comfort, lead, and guide you. If you will just call upon Him, He will answer. He loves you and wants to deliver you from the devil.

In my vision of the seven-headed dragon and the justice scale, I noticed the angels of God fighting against Satan with swords. I saw the Word of God in action, and the angels took the scale away from the devil. When they seized it, I saw something that resembled a round ball on one end, but as I looked closer, I noticed that it was the earth. Then I saw the angels rip open a round door that was upon the earth. As they opened it, the Lord put His hand inside and yanked out deep roots that had all kinds of sins and perversions dangling from them. Everything evil you could imagine clung to these roots He was pulling from the center of the earth. God was tearing down the seven major kingdoms of false gods.

This warfare against this dragon and his defeat were extremely vital to the spiritual well-being of the people of God. I heard the Spirit of the

Lord say that there are several major powers of evil that fight along with this dragon. So I began to pray and take dominion over them. I commanded them to be bound, and I also commanded that whatever they were trying to destroy would be loosed in the name of Jesus. Deep warfare was taking place against manipulation and sin in the earth—against thievery, lying, murder, stealing, adultery, fornication, hatred, bitterness, and all types of evil.

It really touched my heart because I knew that God was fighting this battle. He wanted to restore the hearts of the fathers to the children and the hearts of the children to the fathers. (See Malachi 4:6; Luke 1:17.) It was exciting to know that God was battling on our behalf. I knew that the imbalance on the scale represented the false gods that had risen up over the earth to teach us lies. I saw the justice scales begin to even out, and I knew that God was going to intervene on this earth to bring back the truth and miracles that had been stolen from us.

I am very happy to let the world know that the powers of darkness have to obey, according to the mighty name of Jesus Christ and by the blood He shed.

10

Jesus, Our Deliverer

Satan's Wrath in the End Time

Just as there is a real place called hell, there is a real place called heaven. The gates of each place lead to very different consequences. The gates of hell lead to eternal torment, pain, and hideousness. In contrast, heaven's gates lead to righteousness, peace, and joy. They lead to the heavenly city, which has no need for the sun because the light of God illuminates it and reveals its glory. (See Revelation 21:23.) Each of heaven's twelve gates is made from a beautiful pearl, and they welcome the children of God to a city of gold. (See verse 21.)

While we still have time, we must respond to God's provision of salvation and forgiveness through Christ. Those who refuse God's offer and are still alive at the end of the age will experience terror both on earth and in hell. During one of my visions of hell, Jesus said, "I want to show you what is going to hit the earth once the church has been taken out."

There will come a time when God will remove the church from the earth and take His people to be with Him. With the removal of the church, the Holy Spirit's restraint of the enemy and his forces will also be removed. (See, for example, 1 Thessalonians 4:15–16; 2 Thessalonians 2:1–12.) Then Satan will pour out his full wrath on the people of the world, before Christ returns.

In this vision, the Lord gave me a glimpse of what the enemy's wrath will be like at this time. As I walked with the Lord, I heard an awful sound. We stopped, and I looked down a huge tunnel. It was round and curved, somewhat like a subway. Far back in the tunnel, I could see fire coming toward us, roaring like a train. When the fire was about fifty feet away from us, it suddenly stopped.

The flames were covering an object, and as I looked at this object more closely, I realized it was a gigantic snake, bigger than a locomotive. It opened its mouth, and a huge tongue stretched forth. It came a few feet from the Lord and me before it stopped and recoiled into the large opening of the tunnel. It continued to approach and then retreat, as flames shot from its mouth and it continued to roar.

"Oh, my Lord," I asked, "what is that?"

He answered, "This serpent shall be released on the earth when My church is called away."

Watching this, I thought, *We need to repent of our sins and turn to Jesus Christ stronger than ever before.* We need to prepare people through the good news of the gospel and warn them of this coming wrath before it is too late for them. God does not want the deception of the devil to lead people to experience eternal death. We have to be wise regarding the devices of Satan and realize that there is a price to pay for dying without repentance toward God. Though we will often go through struggles and challenges in life, we must never allow these difficulties to scare us into giving up on our loving heavenly Father.

> **We must share the good news and warn people of the coming wrath before it's too late.**

"For by grace you have been saved through faith, and that not of yourselves; it is the gift of God" (Ephesians 2:8). Salvation is a gift from God. Not only does He give you this gift, but He also remains committed to your ability to hold on to it through His grace.

Now may the God of peace Himself sanctify you completely; and may your whole spirit, soul, and body be preserved blameless at the coming of our Lord Jesus Christ. He who calls you is faithful, who also will do it. (1 Thessalonians 5:23–24)

Your faith is what saves you, but you do not save yourself—Christ does. Neither does God leave you to your own devices after you receive salvation. God's Word assures you that, in every trying situation, He has already prepared a way of escape for you. (See 1 Corinthians 10:13.)

THE FINAL JUDGMENT OF GOD

In a vision, I saw millions of people before God's throne. Every tribe of every nation was there, and I saw the angels separating the people. I saw record books brought before the Lord. Angels were descending on and ascending from the earth—a sight I have seen many times in visions. This was a vision of the end of time and the judgment of God, as we read about in the Scriptures:

Then I saw a great white throne and Him who sat on it, from whose face the earth and the heaven fled away. And there was found no place for them. And I saw the dead, small and great, standing before God, and books were opened. And another book was opened, which is the Book of

Life. And the dead were judged according to their works, by the things which were written in the books. The sea gave up the dead who were in it, and Death and Hades delivered up the dead who were in them. And they were judged, each one according to his works. Then Death and Hades were cast into the lake of fire. This is the second death. And anyone not found written in the Book of Life was cast into the lake of fire. (Revelation 20:11–15)

God has provided us with deliverance from eternal death through the sacrifice of Jesus Christ on our behalf. We need to respond to God's truth and get back onto the straight and narrow pathway of following Him. He wants us to know that He loves us and that He is there to forgive us.

TWO KINGDOMS—TWO CHOICES

I pray that there will be a new awakening in the body of Christ and that we all will realize that Jesus is truly real. He is coming back for a church without spot, wrinkle, or blemish, which will reign with Him forever. (See Ephesians 5:27; Revelation 5:10; 22:5.) In the meantime, He wants us to experience the miraculous power of His peace upon the earth, and to deliver others from the grip of Satan.

Though the kingdom of darkness often tries to imitate and compete with the kingdom of God, there are vast differences between these two kingdoms that continually stand out. God's kingdom is one of life, light, and love. Satan's kingdom is one of death, darkness, and hatred. God always lets us know our options and gives us the right to decide whether we will choose the enemy's way—which leads to death—or His way—which leads to life.

> **God's kingdom is one of life, light, and love.**

I call heaven and earth as witnesses today against you, that I have set before you life and death, blessing and cursing; therefore choose life, that both you and your descendants may live. (Deuteronomy 30:19)

Which way will you choose? Have you chosen life by making a sincere commitment to following Christ and living for Him in holiness? Will you join Him in engaging in spiritual warfare and bringing deliverance to the captives?

I want to encourage all who choose to follow the Lord, especially in these end times, that you are overcomers in the name of Jesus. You will experience the attacks of the enemy, but you can be spiritually strong for the fight.

BE SPIRITUALLY STRONG FOR WARFARE

When engaging in spiritual warfare, it is essential for us to understand what it means to have a proper relationship with Jesus Christ. Many Christians suffer from frustration because they feel helpless to defeat the devil as he raises havoc in their lives through intimidation and condemnation. You can overcome the enemy's strategies by knowing your authority as a child of God and a coheir with Christ. (See Romans 8:17.) Your deliverance can be taken from you only if you *decide* to relinquish your spiritual rights.

Strong against Intimidation

One of the devil's strategies is to inflict enough strife upon you to force you to surrender before realizing the authority you have to defeat him. Demonic spirits are sent out on various assignments against us based on our faith in Christ. This is why those who truly believe God often face trials that are much more strenuous than the ones others experience. One difficulty seems to follow another, because it is the strategy of demonic forces to weigh us down with so much at once that we willingly relinquish our confession of faith and our trust in God.

Do not fall for these deceptive tactics. Regardless of how many attacks the devil may attempt to launch against you, you do not have to succumb to them. God is faithful, and He will not allow you to go through anything that you are incapable of bearing. When the weight of the struggle becomes too heavy, He will provide a way of escape. When you are in proper relationship with Jesus Christ, living in His salvation and authority, He strengthens you when you are weak and empowers you for warfare, delivering you from the gates of hell.

Through Christ Jesus, you hold the power to defeat every foe the enemy sends on assignment against you. It is your heritage as a believer in Christ Jesus to walk in liberty and power and to have victory over the devil's devices. No matter how vigilantly he attacks, remember that no weapon that he forms against you will prosper.

> *"No weapon formed against you shall prosper, and every tongue which rises against you in judgment you shall condemn. This is the heritage of the servants of the LORD, and their righteousness is from Me," says the LORD.* (Isaiah 54:17)

Continually submit to God's will and never allow your life to be steered by fear due to the threats of the devil. In the book of 1 Kings, we read that the wicked Queen Jezebel sought the life of Elijah the prophet because she was enraged by the news that he had killed her false prophets. She sent a messenger to relay a threat to Elijah: *"So let the gods do to me, and more also, if I do not make your life as the life of one of them by tomorrow about this time"* (1 Kings 19:2).

Despite having seen great exploits and miracles from the Lord, this threat from Jezebel consumed Elijah, and he ran for his life into the wilderness where he sat under a Juniper tree and requested to die. (See verses 3–4.) Even when you flee in fear, however, God knows how to find you and restore you to your senses. Later, Elijah was found hiding in a cave when the Spirit of the Lord came and asked him, *"What are you doing here, Elijah?"* (v. 9).

> The safest thing to do in times of uncertainty is to run toward God.

Where would God find you if you fled in fear? The worst place to flee is the dark confinements of your old habitat—your old ways of living. The safest thing to do in times of uncertainty is to run toward the voice of God so you may receive knowledge, wisdom, and strength for living life, and living it more abundantly. (See John 10:10.)

Therefore, as Satan gives orders to hell's gates to destroy your family, finances, mentality, health, or even your faith, you have the authority to counteract his evil devices by applying the Word of God. The Spirit of God will speak to you in a *"still small voice"* (1 Kings 19:12), as He did for Elijah, and give you the instructions you need in order to have victory, especially when you have yielded yourself to the Lord through fasting and prayer. God does not always speak to us with thunder; it is often much more subtle.

For instance, perhaps you are daydreaming as you are driving home from work. You accidentally take a wrong turn, so you decide to take an alternate route home. You later learn that the driver of a large tanker forgot to put his truck in park, and it rolled through the very intersection you would normally take at that time and crashed into a wall. God allowed you to daydream for a few seconds so you would respond to His prompting to take the alternate route. At the time, you thought it was a mistake. Later, however, you rejoiced as you realized God was protecting your life from tragedy.

Strong against Condemnation

Another of the devil's strategies is accusation and condemnation. When the devil sets out to judge you unjustly, he already knows that he is overstepping his bounds. (See Revelation 12:10–11.)

Nevertheless, his trick is to deceive you into bowing down to his gruesome threats.

When the devil spews railing accusations against you, know that these deceitful charges are immediately dismissed because Jesus has already given Himself for our sins. *"Who gave Himself for our sins, that He might deliver us from this present evil age, according to the will of our God and Father"* (Galatians 1:4). In Romans 8:1, Paul wrote, *"There is therefore now no condemnation to those who are in Christ Jesus, who do not walk according to the flesh, but according to the Spirit."* As we confess our sins and keep our relationship with the Lord current, He validates and strengthens us so that we may be presented *"blameless in the day of our Lord Jesus Christ"* (1 Corinthians 1:8).

LIVING IN DELIVERANCE AND VICTORY

Finally, we must recognize that there is not just one method of conducting spiritual warfare and obtaining deliverance that we apply to every circumstance. At times, spiritual warfare simply means taking a strong stand against wrongdoing. At other times, it means remaining silent and trusting God when the temptation to scream in frustration is begging you to give in to it. Sometimes, it means spending a night in intercessory prayer or casting out demons. The real issue in spiritual warfare is not so much a specific form of engagement. Rather, it is the *effectiveness* of the engagement as you are guided by the Holy Spirit in doing what is appropriate for a particular situation.

Though the methods of spiritual warfare may vary, these guidelines and principles will steer you toward deliverance and victory:

- Know your God, and make sure the devil knows that you know God as well.

- Recognize the times we are living in and realize that the devil's assaults will increase against those who belong to God.

- Understand that the devil always makes your situation look worse in the natural than it is in the Spirit. Don't allow mere temporal manifestations to cause you to give up. Ask God for spiritual insight and discernment. *"We do not look at the things which are seen, but at the things which are not seen. For the things which are seen are temporary, but the things which are not seen are eternal"* (2 Corinthians 4:18).

- Realize that you have authority through Christ Jesus, and do not be afraid to exercise that authority to make way for your deliverance.

- Understand that you need to apply God's Word to your life in all situations and to claim His promises.

- Know that you do not have to live the rest of your life bound by a generational curse. You hold the power to rebuke whatever has cursed your life and to be set free by the power of God.

- Recognize that it is not by your own power that you wage spiritual warfare; it is by the Spirit of God that you walk in authority with signs following. (See Zechariah 4:6; Mark 16:20 KJV.)

- Know that though you wrestle in the spiritual realm (see Ephesians 6:12), the battle has already been won for you if you believe in Christ's provision and victory!

If you believe in the Lord Jesus Christ and ask Him to come into your heart, He will not turn a deaf ear to your cry but will rush to deliver you.

A PRAYER FOR COMPLETE DELIVERANCE

Jesus proclaimed in the Word of God,

If two of you agree on earth concerning anything that they ask, it will be done for them by My Father in heaven. For where two or three are gathered together in My

name, I am there in the midst of them.
(Matthew 18:19–20)

Will you allow Bishop Bloomer and me to agree with you in prayer for your complete deliverance?

Father, we pray right now, in the name of Jesus, that the person holding this book will be touched by the power of God. We come in agreement that his/her life will forever change for the better and that every generational curse that has been suffocating his/her destiny will be destroyed in the name of Jesus. We pray that every burden will be yanked from this reader's neck and that he/she will enjoy liberty and freedom of life through Jesus Christ. Father, touch this reader's heart to feel the love of Christ as never before. No longer will he/she walk in fear; may the boldness of the Lord rise up from within this person. Allow him/her to see himself/herself through Your eyes, and may the anointing that destroys every yoke become an everlasting part of his/her spiritual existence. We pray, dear God, that you would release your angels to protect, keep, and lead him/her in the way of righteousness. Deliver this person from the secret bondages that are stagnating his/her spiritual, physical, mental, and emotional well-being. Allow Your favor and Your power to be this reader's portion, today and forevermore, in Jesus' name. Amen.

Always remember—Jesus is your Deliverer!

But I am poor and needy; yet the LORD thinks upon me. You are my help and my deliverer. (Psalm 40:17)

The LORD is my rock and my fortress and my deliverer; my God, my strength, in whom I will trust; my shield and the horn of my salvation, my stronghold. (Psalm 18:2)

And do not lead us into temptation, but deliver us from the evil one. For Yours is the kingdom and the power and the glory forever. Amen. (Matthew 6:13)

About the Authors

Mary K. Baxter

Mary K. Baxter was born in Chattanooga, Tennessee. While she was a girl, her mother taught her about Jesus Christ and His salvation. Although she felt called by God at that time, she was truly born again when she was a young woman and God revealed Himself to her as Savior at the same time He miraculously healed her newborn child.

In 1976, while she was living in Belleville, Michigan, Jesus appeared to her in human form, in dreams, visions, and revelations. During those visits, He revealed to her the depths, degrees, levels, and torments of lost souls in hell, telling her that this message is for the whole world. Since that time, she has received many visitations from the Lord. In God's wisdom, to give balance to her message, she has also received many visions, dreams, and revelations of heaven, angels, and the end of time.

On Mary's tours of hell, she walked with Jesus and talked with many people. Jesus showed her what happens to unrepentant souls when they die and what happens to servants of God when they do not remain obedient to their calling, go back into a life of sin, and refuse to repent.

Mary was ordained as a minister in 1983 at a Full Gospel church in Taylor, Michigan, and recently received a Doctor of Ministry degree from Faith Bible College, Independence, Missouri. Ministers, leaders, and saints of the Lord around the world speak very highly of her and her ministry. The movement of the Holy Spirit is emphasized in all her services, and many miracles have occurred in them. The gifts of the Holy Spirit with demonstrations of power are manifested in her meetings as the Spirit of God leads and empowers her.

Mary, a mother and grandmother, loves the Lord with everything she has—all her heart, mind, soul, and strength. She is truly a dedicated handmaiden of the Lord, and she desires above all to be a soulwinner for Jesus Christ. From the headquarters of Divine Revelation, Inc., her Florida-based ministry, this anointed evangelist continues to travel the world, speaking at conferences, seminars, and other gatherings and telling her story of heaven and hell and her revelatory visits from the Lord.do not remain obedient to their calling, go back into a life of sin, and refuse to repent.

For speaking engagements, please contact:
Evangelist Mary K. Baxter
Divine Revelation, Inc.
P.O. Box 121524
West Melbourne, FL 32912-1524
mkbaxter@mbaxter89@cfl.rr.com
www.mbaxterdivinerevelation.org

ABOUT THE AUTHORS

GEORGE G. BLOOMER

B ishop George G. Bloomer is the founder and senior pastor of Bethel Family Worship Center, a multicultural congregation in Durham, North Carolina, and The Life Church in Goldsboro, North Carolina. He can be seen weekly on his national television broadcast, *Spiritual Authority.*

A native of Brooklyn, New York, Bloomer overcame difficult personal challenges, as well as a destructive environment of poverty and drugs, and he uses those learning experiences as priceless tools for empowering others to excel beyond their seeming limitations. He travels extensively as a conference speaker, and he conducts many seminars dealing with relationships, finances, stress management, and spiritual warfare.

Bloomer is the author of a number of books, including *Looking for Love, More of Him, Authority Abusers, Spiritual Warfare,* and the national best seller, *Witchcraft in the Pews.* He has previously collaborated with Mary K. Baxter on *A Divine Revelation of Deliverance* and *A Divine Revelation of Prayer.*

He has appeared as a guest on several television, radio, and media outlets nationwide, including CNN's *Faces of Faith*, The Trinity Broadcasting Network, *The Harvest Show* (LeSEA Broadcasting), and *The 700 Club* (Christian Broadcasting Network).

Bishop Bloomer has been awarded an honorary Doctor of Divinity degree from Christian Outreach Bible Institute. He resides in Durham with his wife and two daughters.

As surely as the absence of authority produces chaos, the abuse of authority produces destruction. Tragically, it's inside the church—where salvation and love should abound—that some of the worst authority abuse takes place. God's design has been misunderstood, twisted, and manipulated, leaving innocent people as victims and prisoners of controlling, abusive situations. Wake up! This is not God's design for the church—or for authority. Discover the key to breaking free from the bondage of spiritual abuse.

Authority Abusers
(revised and expanded edition)
George Bloomer
ISBN: 978-1-60374-046-3 • Hardcover • 208 pages

Witchcraft in the Pews
(revised and expanded edition)
George Bloomer
ISBN: 978-1-60374-033-3 • Hardcover • 224 pages

As Satan's diabolical schemes have grown more intense, his reach has infiltrated America's pulpits and pews. Discover how some ministers use intimidation and fear against their own congregations. Find out how to resist controlling and abusive authority figures. Grow in your discernment as you get free and stay free in Jesus Christ. It's time for the church to take a stand and position itself for the victory that Christ has already won!

WHITAKER
HOUSE

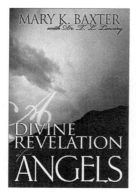

Mary Baxter describes dreams, visions, and revelations of angels that God has given her. Explore the fascinating dynamics of angelic beings—their appearance, their assigned functions and roles, and how they operate, not only in the heavenly realms, but also in our lives here on earth. God's holy angels are His messengers and warriors sent to assist, protect, and deliver us through the power of Christ.

A Divine Revelation of Angels
Mary K. Baxter with Dr. T. L. Lowery
ISBN: 978-0-88368-866-3 • Trade • 288 pages

A Divine Revelation of the Spirit Realm
Mary K. Baxter with Dr. T. L. Lowery
ISBN: 978-0-88368-623-2 • Trade • 208 pages

Mary Baxter gives a unique perspective into the angelic and demonic realms. In vivid detail, she describes her encounters with spiritual beings, both good and bad, as she shares anointed insights into conducting spiritual warfare. This is the strategy manual for spiritual warfare!

WHITAKER
HOUSE

Over a period of thirty days, God gave Mary Baxter visions of hell and commissioned her to tell everyone to choose life. Here is her account of the place and beings of hell contrasted with the glories of heaven. It is a reminder of the need each of us has for the miracle of salvation.

A Divine Revelation of Hell
Mary K. Baxter
ISBN: 978-0-88368-279-1 • Trade • 224 pages

A Divine Revelation of Heaven
Mary K. Baxter with Dr. T.L. Lowery
ISBN: 978-0-88368-524-2 • Trade • 208 pages

After thirty nights of experiencing the depths of hell, Mary Baxter was shown the realms of heaven. Included in these fascinating pages are her descriptions of the order of heaven, angels at work, and the throne of God. These breathtaking glimpses of heaven will turn your heart toward the beauty and joy that await every believer in Christ.

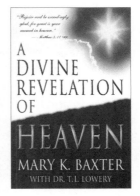

WHITAKER
HOUSE

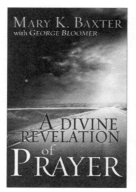

Mary K. Baxter shares eye-opening visions and revelations on the power of prayer. Her remarkable personal answers to prayer will help you overcome fears and failures, receive healing and freedom from addictions, and discern clear direction from God. Experience life-changing breakthroughs in prayer today!

A Divine Revelation of Prayer
Mary K. Baxter with George Bloomer
ISBN: 978-1-60374-050-0 • Trade • 256 pages

A Divine Revelation of Healing
Mary K. Baxter with George Bloomer
ISBN: 978-1-60374-117-0 • Trade • 224 pages

Join Mary K. Baxter as she relates many dramatic, real-life testimonies of people who have received miraculous healing from deadly diseases, illnesses, and destructive lifestyles and habits. Witness the power of God's love at work. Discover how you, too, can walk in divine health and be an instrument of God's healing to others.

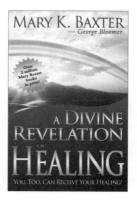

WHITAKER
HOUSE